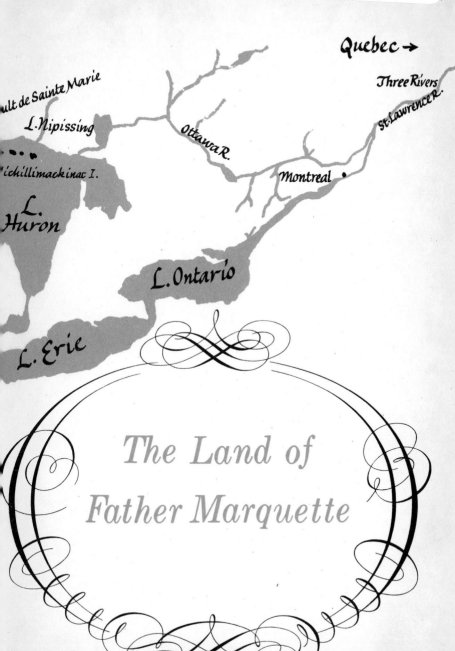

Quebec →

Three Rivers

St. Lawrence R.

ult de Sainte Marie

L. Nipissing

Ottawa R.

Montreal

Michillimackinac I.

L. Huron

L. Ontario

L. Erie

The Land of Father Marquette

FATHER MARQUETTE
and the
GREAT RIVERS

FATHER MARQUETTE
and the
GREAT RIVERS

by

August Derleth

Illustrated by H. Lawrence Hoffman

VISION BOOKS

FARRAR, STRAUS & CUDAHY

New York

Vision Books
is a division of
Farrar, Straus & Cudahy, Inc.

Manufactured in the U. S. A. Published simultaneously in
Canada by Ambassador Books, Ltd., Toronto

Nihil obstat:

John M. A. Fearns, S.T.D.

Censor Librorum

Imprimatur:

✠ Francis Cardinal Spellman

Archbishop of New York

Contents

I. QUEBEC   11

II. THE FIRST MISSION   29

III. FLIGHT FROM THE SIOUX   47

IV. ST. IGNATIUS   65

V. INTO THE UNKNOWN   83

VI. ON THE GREAT RIVER   99

VII. DOWN THE MISSISSIPPI   121

VIII. FACES NORTH   137

IX. BACK TO ST. FRANCIS XAVIER   155

X. THE LAST MONTHS   171

FATHER MARQUETTE
and the
GREAT RIVERS

1

Quebec

AT LAST it was the turn of the seventh ship to come into the port of Quebec. From his place at the rail, Father Jacques Marquette watched the ship turn in the great harbor and move gently in toward shore. It seemed to him that he had waited and prayed all his life for this moment. Finally he was coming to the Canadian missions.

There were many people on the shore. Everything there was bustle and haste, for other ships had unloaded ahead of the one on which Fr. Marquette had sailed from the far country of France.

Back from the shore, the old walled city of Quebec rose on a high rock. How strange it was to see a town in the heart of this wilderness! Along the St. Lawrence, the ship had moved between two walls of forests. Once in a great while there had been houses to be seen, but not until the ship reached Quebec did Fr. Marquette see such a cluster of homes.

Quebec made Fr. Marquette think of the towns of France he had left behind: Laon, where he was born; Nancy and Pont-à-Mousson, where he had gone to the Jesuit schools; Rheims, Charleville and Langres, where he had been a student, a novice, and at last a priest. Quebec too was a French town. It was closely packed, with narrow streets and tight-fitting little houses, except for two. No one had to tell Fr. Marquette that these would be the houses of the governor and his highest officer.

He recalled his mother and remembered the little scene which had been the turning point in his life. He had been reading the accounts which the Jesuit fathers had had printed. They were the stories of their courage and bravery as missionaries among the Indians in New France. He could still see in his heart the window at which he had sat. He could still hear his mother coming up behind him. He could hear again her voice.

"Jacques—why do you not play, like the other boys?" she had asked.

"Because I like to read, Mama," he replied.

"Books are good, but you should play, too. What is it you read? So—again the book about the Jesuits."

"Yes, Mama." Then, looking into her eyes, he knew he must tell her what was in his heart. "Mama, I have made up my mind what I want to be when I grow up."

"So?" she questioned.

"I want to be a missionary," he announced. "I want to go to New France and bring the Indians to God."

She had looked at him long and earnestly. At last she had said, "You are sure, Jacques?"

"I am sure, Mama."

And he had never wavered in his decision. He had never once regretted it.

But now the ship was in port. The captain was shouting orders. Shouts came from shore and flew back from the ship. The gangplank came from the ship's side like a great tongue. It swung out and lowered to the dock. A dozen hands reached up to take hold and secure it.

As he made ready to go down the gangplank, Fr. Marquette murmured a prayer of thanksgiving to the Blessed Virgin, through whose aid he had gained his wish—to be sent to New France, perhaps to labor among God's red-skinned children.

A fellow Jesuit waited for him on the dock. With him was a young fellow, scarcely more than a lad. This boy took Fr. Marquette's baggage at once.

"Father Marquette?" asked the priest. "I'm Father Dablon. This is Louis Joliet, who works among us. We'll take you to the Father Superior. Did you have a good journey?"

"As God willed it," said Fr. Marquette.

Fr. Dablon smiled. "You mean it was rough and

uncomfortable. It's only eleven years since I came over myself. They haven't found a way to make the journey easier."

Fr. Marquette laughed.

Joliet smiled, but did not speak.

They began to climb a steep path. It wound up the face of the slope to the walls of the town. Soon they entered the town. As they went along, Fr. Dablon pointed out the soldiers' barracks, then a great warehouse for furs, a church, a hospital, and a convent of Ursuline Sisters.

The men made a strong contrast. Joliet was just a lad, but he seemed to be bright and alert. Fr. Dablon's robe could not hide his heavy build. He was big and brawny. Fr. Marquette was short and almost thin. He looked to be as lacking in strength as Fr. Dablon was full of it. Fr. Dablon's face was strong and pleasant. Fr. Marquette looked serious. His face was round, with large brown eyes, heavy eyebrows, a high forehead, and a soft mouth.

"If you've been here eleven years," said Fr. Marquette, "you must have been in the missions, Father."

"Oh, yes," replied Fr. Dablon. "I was at Onondaga. I worked among the Cree Indians at Hudson's Bay. I've been up and down the St. Lawrence these last few years. I'll be going out again. That's what we're here for."

At last they came to the big gray building which belonged to the Jesuits.

"Well, here we are," said Fr. Dablon. "Father Superior is expecting you."

Joliet smilingly bade Fr. Marquette farewell and went off down one of the halls of the building.

Fr. Dablon led the way to Father Superior François Le Mercier's quarters. He knocked gently on the door and said, "Father Marquette has come."

"Send him in," came a cheery voice from behind the door.

Fr. Dablon threw open the door for Fr. Marquette and stood aside. He did not follow the newcomer from France into the room.

Fr. Le Mercier got up from his desk and came forward to meet Fr. Marquette. He was a man of sixty years or more, with graying hair and merry eyes. He wore a broad smile.

"We are happy to welcome you among us, Father Marquette," he said.

"It was my life's ambition to come to the missions in New France, Father," answered Fr. Marquette.

And, indeed, he spoke only the simple truth. As he explained to Fr. Le Mercier, he had hoped and prayed to be sent to carry the Faith among the Indians, ever since, as a boy, he had read about the hardships of life in New France. When he had read of the sufferings of the missionaries—the cold, the hunger, and often, the terrible tortures of those priests who were martyred by the Indians, he had dreamed of the day when he too might be sent to Canada. He longed to reach the perfection of his Faith through martyrdom.

Fr. Marquette had tried to pattern his life on that of St. Francis Xavier, who had brought the Faith to Asia. He had waited a long time for his chance to carry the Faith to the Indians of Canada. In those years he had studied and learned many languages, so that he would be ready to learn the Indian languages when he came to New France. But again and again he was passed over by his superiors. Other priests were sent instead. He had prayed daily to the Blessed Virgin of the Immaculate Conception that he be sent, too. And now, at last, his prayers had been heard. He said that he was ready to start at once for any post among the Indians.

Fr. Le Mercier shook his head. A patient little smile came to his lips. "We are well pleased with your willingness, Father," he said. "But all is not as easy as you think. It is good to know many languages, but the Indians speak languages that are very different from the ones you have learned in France. They must be studied long and hard for the best results. And before you go among the Indians, you must learn enough of their talk so that you can speak with them a little.

"Many of our brothers have failed to learn the languages. Many have gone back to France. Others work only among the French."

"I will learn their languages," promised Fr. Marquette.

"If determination will help, I'm sure you will," agreed Fr. Le Mercier. "But, first—you must be very tired. Rest now for a little while, a week or two. Then we shall find a place for you. Do not be anxious. What lies before you will tax your strength, Father."

So he was dismissed. Fr. Dablon waited outside to lead him to the cell-like room which was to be his until Fr. Le Mercier decided where he was to go.

Fr. Marquette waited three weeks. During those weeks, he heard many stories of the Indians. He learned how Fr. de Brébeuf and Fr. Lalemant had been tortured to death by the terrible Iroquois. He heard the story of Fr. Isaac Jogues, who had escaped from the Iroquois only to be killed by the Mohawks. These tales did not dampen his eagerness to be among the Indians. Fr. Marquette did not fear danger. He was clothed in his Faith and filled with the hope of saving many Indian souls. With such a hope, no danger could be too great.

On the evening of October ninth of that year,

which was 1666, word was brought to him to be ready to leave next morning. He packed his few belongings joyously and made ready to go into the wilderness.

But his hope of going to a mission at once was not fulfilled. This he learned when he saw Fr. Le Mercier the next morning.

"We are sending you to the trading post at Three Rivers, Father," he said. "There you will study with Father Gabriel Druillettes. He will teach you the language of the Montagnais, a tribe related to the Algonquins. You will be almost eighty miles away from us, and you will not come back here unless the language proves to be too much for you."

Fr. Marquette thanked him, and the two men bade each other farewell.

Young Louis Joliet walked with Fr. Marquette to the water's edge. He told him that Three Rivers was one of the oldest settlements in New France. It was a rough post, not like Quebec. He would see many Indian and French fur traders there. The St. Lawrence River flowed past it, and the St. Maurice

River came in from the north at that place. Joliet said he had been there.

"I have been many places, Father," said Joliet. "I began by wanting to become a Jesuit too, but now I have decided to become an explorer instead."

When they came within sight of the water, Fr. Marquette looked in vain for the ship. "Where is the ship?" he asked.

Joliet laughed heartily. "Forgive me, Father. You've seen the last of ships for a long time. Who knows? Perhaps forever. You go by canoe."

Even as Joliet spoke, Fr. Marquette saw the canoe waiting for him. It was large enough to hold many supplies, as well as three other men. All were men who worked for the Jesuits. They were waiting impatiently for him.

Fr. Marquette bade Joliet farewell. Then he stepped into the frail boat.

"God be with you, Father," called Joliet.

Then the canoe pushed out into the water, and soon Quebec began to fade into the horizon.

Once Quebec was behind them, only the river and the woods lay around them. Now Fr. Marquette felt that he was truly in the wilderness. The tall pines were still green, but many other trees had begun to turn color. Thousands upon thousands of strange birds flew overhead. Once a flock so large that it shut out the sun went by. These were passenger pigeons, one of the men told Fr. Marquette. Sometimes deer darted away from the water's edge as they paddled near the shore.

Once in a while they met another canoe bearing down toward Quebec. All the travelers in the other canoe, and all the men in Fr. Marquette's canoe raised their paddles in greeting when they met. If they were close enough, they shouted across the water to one another.

From all sides came the voices of the wilderness —the cries and wing-flappings of birds, the rustling along shore of rabbits, squirrels, and other small animals, the hoof beats of deer, the heavy walking sounds of bears. And always there was the talking of the water, the sound of the paddles, the lapping of the river at the canoe.

Time and again, Fr. Marquette was filled with wonder at the beauty and power of the St. Lawrence River. There was a greatness about it that filled him with peace.

And there was a song of happiness in Fr. Marquette's heart and a prayer of thanks on his lips. Every paddle-stroke brought him closer to his goal —the mission to the Indians.

In the middle of the third day, they reached Three Rivers. This little settlement was on the north bank of the St. Lawrence River.

Fr. Druillettes, who had been sent word of Fr. Marquette's coming, waited for him. He was a jolly, fat man. He had been at this post for many years, because he knew more Indian dialects than most of his fellow Jesuits. This knowledge made him useful to Indians and traders alike. At the same time he served his Faith among the savages at and near the post.

Compared to Quebec, Three Rivers was rude indeed. It was truly a town on the edge of the unknown country to the west. The few missions and the trading posts were the only places where white men trod among their red brothers. All its cabins and shops were built of logs. Where it had fortifications at all, they were made from the trunks of young trees. These trunks were stuck into the ground and tied together to make a stockade. Only about five hundred people lived here in all, counting Indians.

Almost the first thing Fr. Druillettes said to his guest was, "You don't look very strong, Father."

"I have the will, Father," replied Fr. Marquette.

"Ah, yes," sighed Fr. Druillettes, "but it may take more than will. I am surprised they ever sent you. And the language . . ."

"When do we begin, Father?"

Fr. Druillettes smiled. "You are in a hurry, my friend. This does not get done with overnight. We begin tomorrow. But do not be surprised if you are here with me next year still."

Fr. Marquette's heart sank, but only for a moment. In his eagerness to carry the Faith to the Indians, he was almost questioning the judgment of his superiors. If it were the will of the Lord that he be patient at this rude post, then it was his own will too.

The next day Fr. Marquette began to study the Montagnais language. He soon understood what Fr. Druillettes and Fr. Le Mercier had meant. It had been easy to study other languages in France, but the Indian dialects were different.

"You see, Father," explained Fr. Druillettes, "here we have no grammar to help us. We have no dictionary. The Indians have many ways of saying the same thing. There are no parts of speech we can memorize. The Indians have words which mean certain objects. They also have words which mean groups of objects. Yet these words are not at all alike. They don't even sound alike. What you must do is to memorize words and signs; that is not the way you have learned languages before."

"It can be done," said Fr. Marquette.

"Yes, it must be, if you are to go among the Indians. You must learn to understand it easily and speak it the same way. Indians don't like to repeat their words. They speak once, and that is enough to them. Since they do not really trust us, they are quick to take offense. If you fumble when you speak to them, they may be offended. And when an Indian is offended, it might mean that his anger will flow over. He might strike and kill in anger."

Fr. Marquette studied hard. He had no thought of failure. It was important to him that he learn as much of the Indian speech as he could. How else could he reach his goal?

But how hard it was! How patient he had to be! All the languages he had learned in France did not help him in the least. Many times his patience wore thin, but his prayers helped him keep trying. Even Fr. Druillettes remarked about his unending efforts.

The weeks passed, and the months went by. Now and then Fr. Druillettes took Fr. Marquette along when he went up the St. Maurice River or elsewhere to visit roving bands of Indians and preach to them. Thus Fr. Marquette was able to hear his friend and the Indians talk together.

Slowly but surely, Fr. Marquette learned the language of the Montagnais tribe. But when he had learned it, he found out that there were other dialects he had to learn.

"I was told to teach you the Indian languages

until you receive orders to leave me," said Fr. Druillettes.

But language was not all that Fr. Marquette learned. He studied the Indians at every chance he had. Most of the Indians who came into the post at Three Rivers were Hurons or belonged to tribes of the Ottawas. He soon learned to tell one from another by noticing what they wore. Some tied bands about their hair. Others had feathers in the bands. Some wore beads on their arms. Others did not. Some used paint on their faces and none elsewhere. Some wore paint on their arms and legs and none on their faces.

Fr. Marquette learned to move about without fear among the Indians. He became used to being called *Black Robe* instead of *Father*. That was the way all the Indians spoke of the Jesuits. As the time passed, he learned many things about getting along with Indians. The missionaries had put down many rules which they had learned through the slow, painful way of experience.

When he went to work among the Indians, Fr. Marquette knew that he must accept all their attentions and must show his gratitude. He must even eat their food, which would often taste very bad. He must not show that he did not like the food. He must never trouble Indians with prying questions. He must not allow his prayers to take too long. He must never keep Indians waiting, and he must prepare to take meals only at dawn and twilight, as the Indians did when traveling. He must not show tiredness or discomfort when he traveled with the Indains. Above all, he must not offer to paddle a canoe, for if he did so, the Indians would expect him to paddle all day without stopping.

These and many more rules Fr. Marquette learned as he studied with Fr. Druillettes. Also, he learned six Indian dialects. He could understand them and he could speak them. Fr. Druillettes was proud of his pupil. But always he was shaking his head and complaining that Fr. Marquette did not look strong enough.

Still Fr. Marquette's orders did not come. He began to think that his superior, Fr. Le Mercier, had forgotten him.

2

The First Mission

MORE THAN TWO YEARS passed before orders came
to Fr. Marquette from Quebec. Fr. Marquette
opened Fr. Le Mercier's letter with hands that
trembled with eagerness. He read the letter in but
a few moments and gave it to Fr. Druillettes to
read. Fr. Marquette was directed to leave at once
for the mission at Sault de Sainte Marie.

"To the Sault!" exclaimed Fr. Druillettes, when
he had read the letter. "That's one of our farthest
missions, Father."

"How far?"

"Ten weeks. Perhaps twelve." Fr. Druillettes shrugged. "It all depends on the weather. At least you're stronger now. It's a hard trip. That is in the country of the Ottawas. But, never fear, they're friendly Indians."

Fr. Marquette set out in the morning. With him were two of the Jesuits' helpers and a strong young Canadian named Albert Broussard. This young man had been waiting for a chance to go into the Ottawa country.

For part of their journey, they traveled west on the St. Lawrence River. They had to go as far again as Fr. Marquette had already come from Quebec to Three Rivers. The Jesuits' helpers explained that the route to the Sault was so hard because they could not take the direct way. This lay through the lakes, which connected to the Sault. But part of this route led among the fierce Iroquois Indians. True, the French and the Iroquois had signed a treaty only three years before. Just the same, the Iroquois did not want to see the canoes of the French on Lake Erie. The Iroquois hated the traders, both French and Indians who worked for the French.

Fr. Marquette and his friends were not alone on the journey. Others travelers were going the same way. It was easier to travel with a group of canoes, even though each went about his own business, than it was to go alone. If one went alone, there was no help near in case of accidents. Besides, unfriendly Indians would not be so likely to attack a chain of canoes as one lone craft.

In contrast to the canoe in which Fr. Marquette rode, the others were very colorful. The travelers and traders all painted their canoes in gay colors. They themselves wore very bright clothing, usually red. As they paddled along, they often sang French songs. Then their voices rang along the river, so that it was no wonder that Indians were often seen along the shores. Sometimes these Indians waved to the travelers to come to shore, and when they went, the Indians bartered whatever the travelers might like for cloth or beads or some other trifle.

The distance between the canoes of the travelers and Fr. Marquette's craft grew steadily greater, because the canoe in which he rode was loaded so heavily that its gunwales were always close to the water. They had to carry enough supplies to last for the length of the journey. There was hardly enough room for them to kneel on the rush mats in the position they took to paddle the canoes. At first their way was easy enough, but not far from Three Rivers, the St. Lawrence River widened into a small lake. Once they were through it, they faced many smaller rivers. All these were branches of the St. Lawrence, and all were filled with rapid water. Since they lost sight of the swifter canoes while on the lake, Fr. Marquette was alarmed when they came to the many rivers.

"We have lost them!" he cried.

"Oh, they are somewhere up ahead," said one of the men in his canoe.

Young Broussard grinned. He was no stranger to this country. "All these rivers lead to the same place, back to the St. Lawrence River, Father," he said. "We are bound to catch up to them."

Fr. Marquette felt better. In a few moments, when they were in the rapid water, he had other dangers to face. For they had to move in constant fear that their canoe might be tipped over or washed too full of water. But Fr. Marquette had no fear; he had faith in the Blessed Virgin, who had always protected him.

Just as Broussard had said, they caught up with the other canoes when the rivers once again joined to form the wide St. Lawrence. The travelers had gone to shore to barter with the Indians. The Jesuits' helpers, tired by the rapid water, moved inshore too, and Fr. Marquette had the chance to talk with the Indians.

He found to his delight that they could understand him, as he could understand them. They seemed to him simple savages. They were friendly, but one of them seemed to be worried about the safety of the Black Robe. He kept pointing southwestward and shaking his head.

"Do not go," he said in the Ottawa language. "The Iroquois wait to kill there."

"We are going north," said Fr. Marquette, beginning to feel sure of his Indian speech.

This satisfied the Indian who had spoken, but

others of the tribes there immediately told many tales of the warlike Iroquois, who had taken arms against Hurons and Ottawas many times. The Indians were so eager to talk and trade that Fr. Marquette had a hard time breaking away from them.

Day followed day. Each night they camped only for the hours of darkness. Then they pushed relentlessly on.

At Montreal they left the St. Lawrence River and began to move up the long, winding Ottawa River. The Ottawa, though broad, was not as large as the St. Lawrence, yet its waters were fully as swift. New France was a wild and beautiful country that had many great, swift rivers, thought Fr. Marquette. More than once they had to journey by land around rapids, carrying their canoe. This was making the portage. At each portage, Fr. Marquette wondered anew how a canoe, which seemed to dance on the waters in its lightness, could be so heavy on the shoulders.

They could not travel fast. Against the wild currents and the sudden summer winds and storms, they could seldom manage to make more than three miles an hour. Often it was less than that. Every time a storm came up, they had to go inshore for shelter. Because of these hardships, they lost many hours.

At one point, the paddlers and Broussard lost their way. They forgot where they had to turn into a smaller stream in order to reach Lake Nipissing. Fr. Marquette had to talk to every band of Indians they saw until they found the right river. They went up this river until they could paddle no more. Then they had to go on a portage of several days before they reached Lake Nipissing.

Yet, at last, Lake Nipissing and the forests of that country were behind them. It had taken them many weeks to travel through this country and then to pass among the many islands of Georgian Bay, following the shore where the pine forests rose unbroken. They were able to travel swiftly in Lake Huron and also up the River of St. Mary. This was a crooked, rushing stream, often very wide, which led them to a course of white water which splashed and tumbled over rocks. This, at last, was the Sault.

Above it, on the shore not far from Lake Superior, lay the settlement that was Fr. Marquette's first mission.

Fr. Louis Nicolas waited only for Fr. Marquette to come on shore before leaving the Sault. He stood on the banks to welcome him.

"I am happy to see you, dear Father," he cried. "My canoe is ready, and I am ready. God willing, I will yet be away before the ice."

"I am as happy to be here, Father," replied Fr. Marquette.

"The Sault is one of our oldest posts, Father," said Fr. Nicolas. "The Indians and the traders have met here for many years. Our mission here is twenty-seven years old. It was founded by Father Jogues and Father Raymbault. Father Jogues is dead now—at the hands of the Indians. And Father Menard, who was here for a while, is dead in the wilderness far to the west. But come, you are tired. Food and rest are what you need."

The old priest was hardly away before Fr. Marquette began to make himself familiar with his first mission. He was greatly surprised by the friendliness of the Indians. Unlike the Hurons who had come to Three Rivers, the Ojibwas of the Sault were not suspicious of him. Much to Fr. Marquette's delight, all of them were ready to listen to him preach the word of God.

The Indians often expressed their pleasure in the little chapel of the mission. It was a stout little building. It was decorated with limbs of spruce and hemlock. There was also altar linen. And there were a few pictures—just enough to make the chapel look to the Indians like the house of the God of whom the Black Robes preached.

Fr. Marquette soon discovered that he never said a daily Mass without many Indians there. They came without being bidden. They sent their children to be baptized and taught. Fr. Marquette was happiest at baptism, because he knew that many of the Indian children died young. They could not live the hard life of the Indians. These innocent children, once baptized, went to heaven; their souls were saved.

In one part of the log building which housed the chapel, Fr. Marquette made his home. The land had been cleared not far away. Fr. Marquette found it already planted with beans, corn and pumpkins. Each day the Indians brought him a tasty fish. They called it *atticameg*, but the traders said it was known to them as whitefish.

Fr. Marquette was so comfortable that he wondered how far he must yet go to meet the hardships of his fellow-Jesuits. He had been trained for a harder life. It was his greatest hope that he would not be kept at the Sault very long. But Fr. Marquette was too obedient and patient ever to complain. If it were the will of his superior that he remain here, then here he would remain. But if it were not, he would go gladly.

Fr. Le Mercier must have known of Fr. Marquette's wish to go where he could truly live among the Indians without the protection of the traders. Or perhaps he read between the lines of Fr. Marquette's reports.

For scarcely a year had passed when, one day late in the summer of 1669, Fr. Marquette received orders from Quebec. He was to relieve Fr. Claude

Allouez at the mission at La Pointe du Saint Esprit. La Pointe lay far to the west, along the south shore of Lake Superior. It was the farthermost mission of the Jesuits. Only ten years before, two fur traders, Pierre Esprit Radisson and Medard Chouart, Sieur de Groseilliers, had founded a trading station there. This was the first white man's dwelling on the shores of Lake Superior. Six years later, Fr. Allouez had followed them.

Fr. Marquette made the journey along the south shore of Lake Superior in a month. Snow and ice made the way very hard. He reached La Pointe on the thirteenth of September. There stood Fr. Allouez's little cabin.

Fr. Allouez, aging and ailing, greeted Fr. Marquette with joy. "This is not a mission for an old man," he said. "It needs a young man who is healthy and strong."

"I'm afraid I've grown soft at the Sault, Father," answered Fr. Marquette.

"You'll soon toughen up here, Father. There are a number of Indian villages nearby. They're scattered all over. You'll have to walk to them. The

Indians are of different kinds—Hurons, Ottawas, Kickapoos, Pottawattomies, Ojibwas. Sometimes Indians from other tribes visit here too."

"Are they friendly?" Fr. Marquette asked.

"Some are. Some are not," said Fr. Allouez. "Don't go too far west or you'll meet the Sioux."

"But even the land of the Sioux belongs to this mission, Father," answered Fr. Marquette. "There is no other mission to the west."

Fr. Allouez smiled at the younger man's eagerness for work. "There are limits to even a missionary's time," he said. "They are a week away, deep in the wilderness, in the country of the great river."

"What river is that, Father?" asked Fr. Marquette.

"They have many names for it. I doubt that it is in the lands of New France. But there are other matters to talk about. The great river isn't one of them. The Sioux are more to be feared than you may think. They often come as far as La Pointe. The Ottawas have come to a truce of some kind with these old enemies of theirs. But Indians are often as children. They do not think what they do. The truce is thin."

They talked together long into that first night.

On the following day, Fr. Allouez set out on the dangerous journey to the Sault, where he would spend the winter with Fr. Dablon, who had relieved Fr. Marquette there. Then he would go on to the mission of St. Francis Xavier in the South.

On that same day, Fr. Marquette set out to meet his charges. He followed the plainly marked trails through the forests and swamps. These trails led straight to Indian villages.

Fr. Marquette was familiar with the Indian camps as he had seen them while he was at Three Rivers. But the first village he now came upon was very different from those others. The Ottawas at the Sault lived in great lodges. Indians on the march did not carry any cover and slept in the open. But these Pottawattomies lived in small rounded huts covered over with bark. And the braves did not usually wear any kind of decoration on their heads. Most of them were Christians, Fr. Marquette discovered. But some were not. Sometimes those who were not Christians stood near him and rudely mocked him.

He saw many differences between tribes as he moved among the Indians. The Kickapoos and the Pottawattomies were usually quite friendly. Many of them had become Christians. The Ottawas were divided. Some of them had become Christians. Some had not. Those who had not made no secret of their dislike of him. Of all the Indians, the Hurons seemed to have come farthest along the road toward civilization.

Fr. Marquette knew that he did not have very much time before winter would close in on his mission. Winter would be a long season of snow and bitter cold. It would be a time when he could travel only in case of great need. He had made up his mind to visit all six of the villages in his mission as many times as he could before winter. Yet he had to make sure he would have enough food to last. Some of this he would get from the Indians. Some he would have to find—nuts, game, dried herbs for tea.

By the time the first deep snow lay on the

ground, Fr. Marquette had learned many things about his Indian charges. In each camp, he knew, there were men who did not want him to come at all. They wished him ill. They would like to see him die. These were the medicine men. They had taught the Indians to believe in magic and witchcraft and such false gods as those of thunder, the sun, and the moon. Now they tried in every way to turn their fellow Indians away from the true God.

Fr. Marquette learned also that many of the Indians only pretended to believe in God. But those who truly believed could always be known. They led good lives. They obeyed the commandments. They came to hear him preach. They brought him their children to be baptized. They asked many questions. They wanted to know more about the Great Manitou of the white men. And at the same time they were filled with wonder at the sight of such familiar objects as the clasp-knives Fr. Marquette used, and even his needle and thread.

But Fr. Marquette was interested in more than his duties at La Pointe.

Many times, when he talked to the chiefs in their

villages, he was told that there was a great gathering of Indians a month's journey to the south. They were the Illinois. They lived in two large villages. There were almost ten thousand of them. Sometimes they came as far north as La Pointe. They were friendly. Perhaps Fr. Marquette would like to visit them?

Fr. Marquette was eager to make the long journey. Many nights he thought for hours about the number of converts he might make among them. But did he dare to leave his mission for so long a time without the written permission of his Father Superior? Besides, the way lay through Sioux country.

Fr. Marquette also heard of the great river with much interest. Some Indians called it the Father of Waters. He heard exciting tales of this river from a roving band of Indians who visited the mission. These Indians were some of the strongest and bravest he had seen. But they did not live in villages. They hunted and bartered furs; so they moved from place to place.

These Indians spoke in wonder of the great river.

Their talk excited Fr. Marquette. He knew how anxious France was to spread her lands in the New World to west and south. And he began to hope that he might help his country enlarge its lands at the same time that he added converts to the fold. Perhaps with the help of the Blessed Virgin of the Immaculate Conception he might gain more land for France when he visited the Illinois.

3

Flight from the Sioux

ONE DAY IN THE SPRING that followed that long, cold winter, visitors came to the mission. An Ottawa Indian named Flying Crow came ahead to warn Fr. Marquette. He was a convert who sometimes helped at the mission. Now he came early one morning. He was excited. He told Fr. Marquette that a body of strange Indians were coming from the South.

In a little while other Ottawas came, together with the visiting Indians. They brought the visitors to Fr. Marquette and led one of them forward to introduce him. His name, the Ottawa said, was Spotted Deer. He was an Illinois Indian, and all his friends were from the same Illinois tribe.

Fr. Marquette welcomed him. He spoke to Spotted Deer in all the languages he knew, but Spotted Deer did not understand any of them. Fr. Marquette had to rely on an interpreter who could speak Spotted Deer's language as well as his. Through this interpreter, they had a long talk.

Spotted Deer said that the Illinois lived in two villages a month's journey away. They were in the South and a little to the West. He and his friends had come in peace. They had seen what Fr. Marquette and Fr. Allouez before him had taught the Indians of La Pointe. Now they wished Fr. Marquette to come with them to their villages.

"How many Illinois live in the two villages?" asked Fr. Marquette.

"Close to ten thousand," answered Spotted Deer.

Fr. Marquette had never seen so many Indians at one time. Here indeed was a chance to do great missionary work. Ten thousand souls! Was this not truly part of his mission, as well as La Pointe?

"Come and teach our people," Spotted Deer requested.

Fr. Marquette asked what these Illinois did so far from home.

"We are a hunting party," replied Spotted Deer. "We have traveled for more than a month. We set out from our village on the other side of the great river."

Fr. Marquette was quick to catch what Spotted Deer had said. Once again he heard of the great river. Eagerly, he questioned Spotted Deer. He said he had heard of this river before. But no one could tell him where it was.

Spotted Deer said it was in the country of the Illinois, less than an hour east of their villages. It was a river about three miles wide at that point. It flowed from cold country into hot country, among many strange Indian villages, through places where no snow ever fell and where two crops of Indian corn were raised in one year. It ran from far up in the North, deep into the South.

"Even we who live where it flows do not know where its mouth is," said Spotted Deer.

Fr. Marquette grew excited. Perhaps this great river was at last the long-sought way to the western sea! It did not seem possible that it could empty into the sea at Virginia. Therefore it must go the other way, to the west. Somehow he must see this great river.

"I will come among your people as soon as God wills," he promised Spotted Deer. "But, if your villages are to the west, are you not in the country of the Sioux?"

Spotted Deer admitted that it would be necessary to pass through the country of the Sioux to reach the Illinois villages. He went on to explain that the Sioux and the Illinois were friendly. When his hunting party went back to their lands, they would ask the Sioux for safe passage for Fr. Marquette and for anyone who went with him.

Fr. Marquette was delighted. He gave the Illinois his blessing and parted from them.

He lost no time in getting ready for the task before him. Before he could carry the word of

God to the Illinois, he must learn their language. The Illinois belonged to the Algonquin nation. He already knew a little of the Algonquin language, but not enough. So every day, in what little time he could spare from the work of his missions, from tending his crops and caring for his flock, he studied the language of the Illinois with one of the Ottawas who knew it.

The Illinois under Spotted Deer kept their word. Within a month, a group of Sioux Indians appeared at the mission. They were led by a chief who called himself Grey Cloud. Many of them, like some of the Ottawas, wore furs.

The Sioux were strong, brawny Indians. They were greatly feared by all the Indians of La Pointe, and they seemed to be proud of their reputation for fierceness. An air of uneasiness lay among the other Indians as long as the Sioux were squatted in a half-circle before the mission, talking with Fr. Marquette, again by means of an Ottawa interpreter.

They had come, Grey Cloud explained, because

their friends, the Illinois, had asked safe passage for the priest. They had come to see for themselves what kind of man the Black Robe was. They did not trust any of the Black Robes. They did not understand the priests' talk of a God of love. All they knew was a life of war and fighting. Even so, they were willing to grant Fr. Marquette safe passage through their lands if he would promise not to stop to talk with their people.

Fr. Marquette answered gently, "It is my duty to carry the word of Him who lives in the sky to all who worship false gods. Do not the Sioux worship false gods, too?"

The Sioux did not know what to say. They took council among themselves. They talked angrily and rapidly with many gestures and much shaking and nodding of heads.

Fr. Marquette went into the mission and gathered a few holy pictures for them. He came out and gave these pictures to the astonished Sioux. He told them they were pictures of the Blessed Virgin, the Mother of God, and of Jesus, the Son of God. He explained the Holy Trinity while the

Indians peered closely at the pictures he had given them. They looked upon them as gifts and began to make signs of gratitude.

Finally Grey Cloud said, "It is spoken. The Black Robe shall have safe passage. He need not make promises. He must not bring trouble among the Sioux. That is all."

The Sioux took their leave on this note of friendship.

In the weeks and months that followed, Fr. Marquette studied harder than ever to learn the language of the Illinois. Yet he never neglected his duties. He walked many miles from one Indian village to another, and he stood all the insults of those Indians who resented him and would not listen to him. He preached to his flock once a week and read Mass among them as well as at the mission.

When at last Fr. Marquette felt that he knew the language of the Illinois well enough to be able to make himself understood among them, spring had come again to La Pointe. A year had passed since the visit of Spotted Deer. This was the time he planned to travel into the Southwest to visit the Illinois. He began to make ready for the journey.

Then one day, as Fr. Marquette came toward the village of the Ottawas which was part of his mission, he was astonished to see the Ottawa sentinels turn and run from him. They ran back into the village. Then soon other Ottawas came running toward him. They fell to their knees before him and begged him not to go into the village. He would be displeased and unhappy at what he saw.

Fr. Marquette bravely ordered them to stand aside.

They did so, looking sullen.

He hurried on. As soon as he entered the village, he knew that something unusual was taking place. All the Indians were gathered at the center of the village. This was a large square in front of the cone-shaped lodge of the tribal chief.

Fr. Marquette pressed through the yelling crowd. He saw a double line of Ottawa braves armed with sticks and stones. Another Indian was being forced to run between these two lines.

Every one he passed struck him hard. When he came through the line, the Indian fell to the ground.

Fr. Marquette pushed his way out of the crowd and ran to him. He saw then that the captive was a Sioux brave. He tried to help him up. One of the Sioux's arms had been broken.

Then the priest was seized by both arms and lifted away.

At the same time, the Sioux brave was dragged over to a post rising out of a pile of sticks. The Ottawas meant to burn him alive.

Fr. Marquette shouted in righteous anger. They must not do this thing. This was not the will of God.

The medicine men came dancing toward him. They were dressed in hideous costumes. Their faces were covered with horrible masks of birds and animals. Their feathers and body colors were gaudy. They made scornful gestures at Fr. Marquette.

Then the tribal chief came up to Fr. Marquette and spoke to him angrily. "The Black Robe has no right to interfere with the ancient customs of our tribe," he said. "This is a custom of the Sioux. It is the custom of the Ottawas. Whenever an Ottawa is taken prisoner by the Sioux, this is his fate. The Sioux we capture must meet the same fate. This Sioux is a spy. He must die. I, Dark Moon, have spoken."

The chief made a motion and Fr. Marquette was dragged back, away from the crowd, to the edge of the village. Two braves barred his way. He could not enter the village again until the ceremony had been finished.

Fr. Marquette was sad and bitterly disappointed. Here was another case which showed how easily the Indians returned to savagery. True, some of the Ottawas were not Christians. But Christian and savage stood together in favor of burning the captive Sioux as the tribe had always done. Now Fr. Marquette would have his work to do all over again.

Saddened, he turned and began the journey back to the mission. He was fearful of what would happen when the powerful Sioux nation learned what had happened to one of the Sioux braves in the village of the Ottawas.

Within a week, Fr. Marquette's fears were realized.

He was awakened in the night by a pounding on his door. When he threw open the door, he saw by the light of the candle he carried a half-circle of Sioux Indians. They were led by Grey Cloud.

Fr. Marquette stepped out to meet with them. He stuck the candle he carried into the ground.

The Sioux were menacingly silent. No one spoke a word. Grey Cloud turned and motioned to someone behind him.

An Ottawa brave was pushed forward. He was bound. He fell before Fr. Marquette and lay there until one of the Sioux took him by the hair and raised him to his knees. Fr. Marquette recognized him as White Wing, the son of that very Ottawa chieftain, Dark Moon, who had ordered the burning of the Sioux brave.

Then Grey Cloud began to speak. "We have

come to return the gifts the Black Robe gave to the Sioux," he said. As he spoke, one of his braves came forward and laid the holy pictures on the ground before Fr. Marquette. Grey Cloud went on. "We have promised the Black Robe safe passage. We no longer do so. He must not travel through the Sioux country. Harm may befall him."

"Why have you come to warn me?" asked Fr. Marquette. "Does not the Sioux strike swiftly, without warning?"

"Because you are not our enemy," answered Grey Cloud in a friendlier voice. "Our eyes saw you try to save our brother from the anger of the Ottawas. Now, because you are their friend, we tell you this. We have danced the war dances. We have smoked the war pipe. We will make war upon the Ottawas and the Hurons and all others who are here in this place."

"Is it then too late for a peace talk?" cried Fr. Marquette.

Grey Cloud shook his head. "No peace." Then he added craftily, "But we cannot make war if there are no more of our enemies here. We have spoken."

"I ask one favor," said Fr. Marquette boldly.

"Speak, Black Robe," replied Grey Cloud.

Fr. Marquette pointed to White Wing. "Give him to me."

Grey Cloud was startled. But only for a moment. Then he turned to his braves and explained what the priest had asked. Several of the Sioux braves spoke. Grey Cloud listened to everyone who wished to be heard.

Then he turned back to the priest. With his foot he spurned White Wing. "He is yours," he said. "We have other prisoners to put to the torture. This one we give to you because you tried to save our brother. Farewell, Black Robe."

As he finished speaking, all the Sioux rose silently and faded into the night.

Fr. Marquette bent and unbound White Wing.

At once the Ottawa told Fr. Marquette that he and a party of braves had been ambushed late that day by scouting Sioux. The Sioux had scouts and spies everywhere. They meant to wipe out all other Indians in this part of the country. But the Hurons and the Ottawas still had a chance. If they were to take flight, the Sioux would let them go. Perhaps the Sioux would prefer them to flee. They did not want a war. But no Huron or Ottawa would be left alive on La Pointe if they did not remove themselves from the path of the Sioux.

"Whose was the fault?" asked Fr. Marquette gently.

White Wing hung his head. "It was ours," he admitted. "We ourselves broke the treaty. It was not the Sioux."

Fr. Marquette sighed. "Go to your father, then, and tell him what Grey Cloud said."

Sitting alone in his little room, Fr. Marquette was discouraged. White Wing had gone to his village. His father would call the council of the chiefs. They would talk with the chiefs of other villages, with the Hurons and the Pottawattomies and others.

His sleep that night was sorely troubled.

In less than three days, the tribes had made

their decision. All the villages were to be abandoned. Canoes were being built. Stores of meal and dried fish were being collected. Skins, arms, clothing, the Indians' simple tools, rush mats, and such of their furnishings as they could save were being packed for the long journey into the East.

Scouts had already gone out across Lake Superior to the east toward the Sault. They had been sent to look for a new land where the Hurons and the Ottawas might settle. The Kickapoos and the Pottawattomies were going back to their old lands in the Southeast. The Ojibwas were going less far away to where there were others of their nation.

Fr. Marquette had made many converts, especially among the Hurons. Indeed, almost the entire Huron village had accepted the Faith. Was all this work, then, to be in vain? If he now remained at La Pointe, what would happen to his flock? And where would he find new converts? The Sioux were too far away. The Illinois were now beyond his power to reach. If only he had gone earlier, before the Ottawas had so foolishly broken the truce with the Sioux!

His first thought must always be of his flock, he knew. His hope of the discovery of the great river faded. Perhaps it was not God's will that he add the country of that river to the lands of New France.

Fr. Marquette had little time in which to make his decisions. The Indians were not waiting for the return of the scouts. They would meet them at the Sault. There they would learn what land the scouts had chosen for them to settle upon. If his church and mission here must be abandoned, then it was surely the will of God that it be so. His mission was not in a church, not within four walls. It was among the Indians. Where the Hurons went, there was his mission.

He sent word to the Hurons that he would go in flight with them wherever their chiefs decided to settle. The grateful Hurons in turn helped him pack everything he would need for the building of a new mission elsewhere.

In less than a week they were on the way. The Indians were all badly frightened. The Sioux were fierce fighters, and when they were on the war path they were without mercy. The Ottawas were especially frightened, because it was toward them that the anger of the Sioux was chiefly directed.

Once more Fr. Marquette made his way along the south shore of Lake Superior. The canoes of the Indians made a set of long, straight lines in the water. They traveled as far as they could each day, fearing that the Sioux would show up at any moment on their trail.

Often storms rose suddenly and drove them to shore. Each time this happened, the medicine men performed wild dances to the Thunder God. And the braves and squaws made sacrifices to the waters of Lake Superior by throwing food and clothing into the water, while the medicine men beat drums and shrieked. Then Fr. Marquette led prayers to the true God. Every evening, he put up a rude shelter and said the Mass.

When they reached the Sault, the Huron scouts were not yet there.

But in ten days they came from the Southwest, filled with praise of their old home on the great island of Michilimackinac, far below the Sault, in that place where Lake Huron and Lake Michigan were joined. The Hurons held many councils all that night before they came to a decision.

The next day the Hurons with Fr. Marquette still among them set out down the River of St. Mary for the island of Michilimackinac. There Fr. Marquette was to start his third mission—that of St. Ignatius.

4

St. Ignatius

THE HURONS' GOAL was an island well known to Indians and traders alike. Its high, steep rock could be seen for many miles across the water. It was a meeting place for Indians and traders of all kinds. Long ago, it had been the old home of the Hurons, but the coming of the Iroquois had forced the Hurons to leave this place for La Pointe. Now they were coming back.

But Michilimackinac was no longer what it had been. Now it was crowded with Indians. There were also many more white men. And every winter, the Hurons learned, Indians from as far away as the Sault came to fish here, for fish of all kinds were plentiful.

Fr. Marquette hardly had time to establish his mission before the Hurons showed how dissatisfied they were. There was no room for their fields. If they built up anew all the cone-shaped wigwams they had had to leave behind, they would be crowded upon the villages of other Indians who had settled on Michilimackinac.

After many councils, they decided to move across the straits to the west. Their new home was a point of land jutting out toward Michilimackinac. They were not far away from their old home, but this new place pleased them more. Fr. Marquette went with them, and his converts among the Hurons helped him to build another log church for the new mission of St. Ignatius. Then the Hurons put up a high fence of wooden stakes and a fort to defend their lodges. The Hurons lived more closely together than many other Indians. As many as six Huron families lived in a single lodge. They were separated only by a partition of bark or skin. Fr. Marquette had a lodge all his own, next to the church.

Soon Fr. Marquette was carrying on the matters of his mission again. He visited the Hurons in their lodges and in their fields. He went around among them to call them to prayer because there was no church bell to be rung. He made new converts among other Hurons and Ottawas who moved in to join the growing village at St. Ignatius. He was happy to see that often the Indians came, without being told, to pray in the chapel. Only a few months after the arrival of the first groups of Hurons at St. Ignatius, five hundred Hurons and thirteen hundred Ottawas were living there.

When he sat down that autumn to make his report, he knew that Fr. Le Mercier had been recalled to France and that Fr. Dablon had become the new Father Superior. Perhaps he remembered that Fr. Dablon was as interested as the Governor in adding to the lands of New France.

First he wrote Fr. Dablon of his success among the Hurons.

"Last summer, when I had to go to the Sault with Fr. Allouez, the Hurons came to the chapel all during the two weeks I was gone, and the girls sang the hymns they knew. When I came back, all came from the fields to the chapel to express their joy. I gladly attended their great pumpkin feast and bade them be grateful to God for their plentiful harvest. The hunting this year has been very good. The woods have been full of bears, deer, beavers, and wildcats. There has been no lack of food."

He complained a little about the way the Hurons believed in dreams. "One must work hard to deal with savage minds," he wrote. "They are without knowledge. God alone can give them light and understanding when we tell them of the Faith. It is so easy for them to slip back into the superstitions of their fathers."

But at last he came to that thought which still stayed in the back of his mind. He wrote to Fr. Dablon of the great river.

"I have heard much of a great river which is said to be miles wide. It flows to the southwest of

La Pointe. It is said to be in the country of the Sioux and the Illinois. It is said that is flows far south to a place where the winters are mild and the soil so fertile that two crops a year are raised on it. They say it flows among other savages who trade with white men. And there are men there who pray with rosaries, as we do, and who go to church, called by the ringing of bells. The river is known by an Indian name, *Messipi* or *Messisipi*.

"I had hoped to add the lands of the great river to those of New France when I went among the Illinois. But God willed otherwise. The danger of the Sioux forced us to flee."

In the spring, Fr. Marquette received an answer from his superior.

The great river was not new to Fr. Dablon. He wrote that traders, missionaries, and Indians had brought word of it to Quebec years ago. But he, like Fr. Marquette, could write only from hearsay. He had heard that it circled the Great Lakes and then flowed south into the sea. It was said to be broader ten miles from its mouth than the St.

Lawrence River was at Quebec. Members of some tribes from the South reported that many Indians lived along its shores. All accounts agreed that the great river was very long and very wide, but no one knew where it emptied.

When Fr. Marquette had read Fr. Dablon's letter, he scolded himself for clinging to his dream of finding the great river. Fr. Dablon's letter was proof that many others held the same dream—to set eyes upon the great river, to map and chart its course. Fr. Marquette told himself that he had been dangerously close to the sin of pride. He had almost forgotten that humility was especially pleasing in the sight of God. He resolved to put his dream of finding the great river out of his thoughts and to redouble his efforts among the Indians.

But his resolve was not strong enough to drive out all thoughts of the great river. Compared to the mission at La Pointe, Fr. Marquette had few hardships at St. Ignatius. Perhaps because of this, he had more time to think of the great river. He could not put his hopes and dreams entirely out of his heart.

That spring faded into summer, and summer in turn became autumn.

Then one day late in autumn, visitors came out of the East to see Fr. Marquette. The Hurons, who met every canoe at the water's edge, brought them to the priest's lodge. Fr. Marquette saw a young man whom he was sure he had seen before, together with five sturdy travelers. All were young and brawny. They carried two stout canoes of birchbark with cedar splints and spruce root ribs covered with yellow pitch pine. Both canoes were loaded with supplies.

Their leader presented himself to Fr. Marquette. He took off his hat and smiled. He stood bareheaded in the cold December wind that blew.

"Father Marquette, don't you remember me?" His smile broadened. "I've brought you orders from Father Dablon."

Fr. Marquette's eyes lit with recognition. "Why, it's Louis Joliet!" he cried. "You were just a boy in Quebec when I came. But come in and tell me about the orders you bring."

"They are not only from Father Dablon, but also

from Louis de Buade, Count of Frontenac, Governor of New France, and from Jean Talon, the governor's highest officer, our Intendant at Quebec. You shall see."

Fr. Marquette waited patiently until Joliet could find the orders. Joliet was a grown man now. He must now be twenty-eight, thought Fr. Marquette, eight years younger than he. Joliet's sharp bright eyes and friendly manner had not changed.

At last Joliet succeeded in getting the orders out of his clothes. He handed them to Fr. Marquette.

As he broke the seals, Fr. Marquette could not have guessed what the orders contained. They were short, wasting no words. Fr. Marquette was told to go with Louis Joliet "to discover the great river." Fr. Dablon's letter was one of permission for him to make the trip with Joliet. Fr. Marquette was told to write down an account of his journey for the Jesuit *Relations*, that same work which he had so often read as a boy.

Fr. Marquette closed his eyes as if he could not believe what he had read. But he knew that at last his hope was to be fulfilled. And was this not the direct aid of the Blessed Virgin? For what day was this but her very own—the feast of the Immaculate Conception! At once he resolved that if he found the great river he would name it after the Blessed Virgin of the Immaculate Conception. And so too would he name his first mission among the Illinois.

"And now," said Joliet in a businesslike manner, "we shall have to find quarters for the winter. We'll have these months in which to get ready."

"But why have they chosen me?" asked Fr. Marquette humbly.

Joliet shrugged. "Perhaps because you are known to be cautious and without fear, Father. Perhaps because you have been at three missions and have always been very friendly with the Indians. In each place, you left behind much good will. If these Indians learned to like you, Father, the unknown tribes we must face might also do so. I do not know. You were chosen."

"But there are others better fitted for this journey," protested Fr. Marquette. "I am no woodsman. I am no writer. I am not even a good observer."

"But you have always been interested in the great river. So you were chosen," replied Joliet.

Fr. Marquette was sure that his daily prayers for the help of the Blessed Virgin had been answered. That night he gave thanks for a long time on his knees.

All that winter was spent in preparation. Word of the coming journey was spread by traders and Indians. All those who knew anything of the country in the Southwest stopped at St. Ignatius to talk with Fr. Marquette and Joliet. Every scrap of information from Indians and traders was carefully put down.

The first thing Fr. Marquette discovered was that it would not be necessary to go back to La Pointe to reach the great river. Many Indians reported that it flowed far south of the land of the Sioux as well as through that land. It could be reached if the travelers went down along the lake from St. Ignatius to the long bay and there entered the mouth of a river which might take them close to the great river.

Though the traders laughed at the superstitions about the great river, the Indians thought that it was full of dangers. No Indian believed otherwise. They warned the white men of monsters and savage tribes which they would meet.

Fr. Marquette and Joliet made rough maps of the unknown country which lay ahead. Often the stories told by the Indians varied widely. No two were exactly the same. Yet they agreed about many things, and it was possible for Joliet to draw a map which they believed might help them in their journey.

They repaired the two canoes. These little craft were so light that four men could carry them across any portage to which they came. Their supplies were light, too. They took only Indian corn and smoked meat. For much of their food, they would have to depend on wild game or gifts from the Indians. They had to carry arms, extra clothing, materials for the repair of the canoes in case of accident, and other materials to be used for their maps and reports. These had to be carefully protected against the weather. Besides, they had to take along handmills for grinding meal, cloth, clasp knives, thread, beads, hatchets and other things to be used as gifts for Indians they would meet.

By the time spring came, all was in readiness. Only the ice on the lake was not, and the ice did not leave the lake safe for the light canoes until May. Even then, Fr. Marquette had to wait for the coming of Fr. Philippe Pierson to take charge of the mission of St. Ignatius. But he came in one of the first canoes out of the North, and they were free to go.

On the morning of the seventeenth of May in that year, which was 1673, they set out. Fr. Marquette, Joliet, and Pierre Porteret, one of the paddlers, were in the lead canoe. In the second rode the other four travelers, colorful in their gray homespun coats, their bright red leggings, their red pudding-bag caps, their gay sashes and moccasins.

The Hurons and Ottawas of the mission, wearing skins of fur and decked with feathers, beads, and dyed porcupine quills, lined the shore to bid them farewell. All were saddened by Fr. Marquette's going. They were sure that they would never see him again.

Their course was down the lake. They traveled not far out from shore. Fr. Marquette had placed the voyage under the protection of the Blessed Virgin. He traveled happily, feeling certain that their mission would be fulfilled.

After the long winter, all of the men were happy to be on the water again. They sang as they paddled out of the straits of Mackinac and up along the north shore of Lake Michigan.

All day they moved along without stopping.

That night they drew their canoes up on shore where a forest rose. They had come a long way, and soon they would reach the mouth of a river which would take them to a friendly tribe of Menominees. These Indians knew the Black Robes. Many had become converts. They might also know something of the great river. All six of the travelers sat around the campfire that evening over their supper, making plans for the next day. This was the way it would be on many nights to come.

One morning they came to the river of the Menominees and turned into it. The Menominee village was not a far journey from the river's mouth.

The Indians greeted them in friendship and made them welcome. They offered the travelers food which was made of wild rice. Every autumn the Menominees gathered this grain from its tall stalks which grew in shallow water and swampy places. Fr. Marquette was much interested in this grain and asked many questions about it. Most of the Indian food he had eaten did not taste very good, though he had eaten it without complaint. But the wild rice had a delicate flavor and was free of the fat and grease which were so common in the Indians' food.

After they had eaten, the aged Menominee chief, who was called Looks-Twice-Around, came to talk with them. They sat in a great circle while Fr. Marquette explained that he and his friends were seeking the great river of the West.

As soon as he had finished speaking, the Menominees broke out in a great chattering among themselves. There was much shaking of heads. The braves and the minor chiefs turned their faces away from Fr. Marquette or covered their eyes to show that he was in great danger.

Finally Chief Looks-Twice-Around answered Fr. Marquette. "You must not go on this trip. You must turn back. We know this great river. It is terribly dangerous to go there. On its banks live other Indian nations who show the white man no mercy. They kill without reason. Many of these nations war among themselves.

"Even if you reach the great river in safety, it is not safe to travel on it. The river is filled with peril. It is full of great monsters, who swallow men and canoes. Then there is the great demon of the waters. He can be heard for many miles, roaring in a loud voice. He bars the way and swallows up all who come near him. Even if you escape him, the heat of the great river below is so great you will all be roasted in it. I have spoken."

Joliet laughed heartily, hearing this.

Marquette listened gravely and replied gently, "We thank you, great chief. But we cannot do as you say. Many souls are at stake. I cannot think of my life before the salvation of these poor souls. Each of us must do his duty as He who lives in the sky wills it. I beg your forgiveness, but I do not believe in this demon. We will meet and slay all monsters of the waters. We will be on guard against unfriendly Indians."

Then he prayed with them, and the party returned to the canoes. When the Menominees saw that the white men were going in spite of all warnings, some among them began a strange, wailing chant.

"They do their best to scare us," said Joliet as they pushed down river. "But me, I do not scare easily. And I see you do not either, Father."

"No, I do not," agreed Fr. Marquette. "There is no greater death than martyrdom."

Joliet made no answer to this. "Within a day

or two, we should be in the bottom of the long bay. There is a river there. We must go up that river. Then we will be at the last mission, Father."

Fr. Marquette watched the changing landscape with interest as they went down the great V of the long bay. The western shore, he saw, was grim and forbidding. It was wooded with pine and looked bleak. On the east there were headlands and sharp slopes. Here too trees covered the land. In one place, a long cliff of red clay and sand rose to a height of almost eighty feet. On top of this cliff rose the humpbacked mounds left by Indians who had once lived there.

The water of the bay was wild. Cross-winds and cross-tides made it stormy. It was difficult indeed to paddle through this stretch of water, which the travelers called Death's Door. The canoes made their cautious way down the western shore, as they neared the bottom of the bay.

But at last the travelers came within sight of the mouth of the Fox River. It was almost hidden by the great marshes of wild rice that choked it. Flocks of geese, wading birds, wild ducks and river ducks flew up in great clouds at their approach. All had been feeding among the reeds and wild rice along the shore. The river's mouth was very wide, but not far from its mouth, it grew narrow, and a rocky rapids challenged them.

Beyond this lay the mission of St. Francis Xavier, and some miles on the far side of this last Jesuit mission in this wilderness was the village of the Mascoutens, who were known as the Fire Nation.

5

Into the Unknown

THE MISSION of St. Francis Xavier had been established by Fr. Allouez after he left La Pointe. The little mission chapel and the adjoining place for the priest to live were only a few miles up the Fox River from the lake. The mission was surrounded by an Indian village. Fr. Louis André was in charge of the mission, which stood on high ground away from the rocky rapids of the river.

Fr. André took the travelers to his little cabin.

He was eager to hear of their adventures and wanted to know their plans.

As soon as he had heard them, Fr. André said, "You'll need guides to take you up the Fox River beyond the long lake. The wild rice patches are so thick on the upper Fox River that many times it is hard to find the channel."

"Can we get guides from among the Indians here?" asked Fr. Marquette.

"It would be better to get them at the village of the Mascoutens at the head of the long lake."

He went on to say that the Indians both at his mission and in the village of the Fire Nation were all friendly. The Miamis, who lived with the Mascoutens, were the smartest of the Indians. When Fr. Allouez had been among them, they had given him very little rest. They liked to hear him preach so well that they often insisted he go on talking, even during the night. The Kickapoos also lived with the Mascoutens, and along the way were little groups of Fox and other Indians. All these Indians were good hunters, and game was very plentiful everywhere.

They rested two days. Then they started up the Fox River.

Their course was broken by many rapids where the water tumbled over sharp rocks. The portages were made over rocky country too, so that often their feet were cut. Between the shallow, rocky places in the river lay deep water. The Fox River flowed through beautiful country of high, steep banks and wooded lands. Sometimes the shores were dark with trees. Often there were little settlements of Indians to be passed, and at each of them the Indians came to the shore to watch them go by.

On the second day out of the St. Francis Xavier mission, they made a final portage at an island, and came out upon the long lake. Fr. Allouez had called it the Lake of St. Francis, but the Indians knew it as the Lake of the Winnebago. The lake lay in flat country, and the Fox River flowed through this great body of water. The lake's edge was green with wild rice. The shore line could hardly be seen for all the green rushes along it.

They pushed steadily across the lake. Soon the place of their entrance was lost in the horizon behind them. Up ahead, there was nothing but a broad stretch of water. Yet somewhere there was still the Fox River, winding its way toward its juncture with the broader river which must carry them to their goal, the great river.

It was nightfall before they came out of the lake.

At the place where the Fox River entered into the lake rose half a dozen wigwams. There Fr. Marquette asked where he might find the Fire Nation. He learned that it was not far away. They could reach it that night or early next day, as they wished. But they must know that it did not stand on the shore of the river, but more than two miles from it. The place was plainly marked.

It was the seventh of June when they came to the village of the Mascoutens, a large settlement surrounded by a high fence of wooden stakes. The first sight of these Indians gladdened Fr. Marquette's heart, for he saw a great cross standing in the middle of their village. When he came close to it, he saw that it was hung with skins, belts, bows and arrows. These were the Indian offerings to the Great Manitou, which was their name for God.

The village stood on a little rise in the land. Prairies flowed away on all sides. They were broken by groves of tall trees and fields of Indian corn. The Mascoutens all lived in a kind of dwelling Fr. Marquette had not seen before. This was one made not of bark, but of rushes.

The Mascoutens, the Miamis, and the Kickapoos were all friendly. Yet they watched Fr. Marquette as if they had never seen a Jesuit before. They had the curiosity of wild creatures. Some followed him and paid him so much attention that he was glad when he could free himself from them by going to the lodge of the chief, an old man named Green Tree.

As soon as Fr. Marquette explained their need for guides, Chief Green Tree called a council of all the chiefs. He sent runners among the Indians, and soon all the chiefs had gathered near his lodging. They sat in the usual half-circle, waiting to hear from Green Tree and the travelers.

First Chief Green Tree spoke. "Our white

brothers have come among us in need," he said. "Listen to them."

Joliet then got to his feet and told them he had been sent out by the Governor of New France to discover new countries. He pointed to Fr. Marquette and said, "The Black Robe has been sent to bring the Word of God to all God's red children. The Black Robe is a great man. He speaks for Him who lives in the sky. He is not afraid to die in the service of God."

The chieftains were impressed. They nodded their heads and made grunting sounds to show their approval and admiration.

Then Joliet gave them presents and spoke again. "We seek the great river," he said. "Our need now is for guides to show us the way up the river to the place of the crossing. We have heard tales that the river on which we came leads to another river. And we were told that this other river in turn leads us to the great river, for it flows into it. We ask your help in finding our way."

When he sat down, Chief Green Tree rose again. "You have heard our white brothers. They will stay with us for two days. When they go again on their journey, they wish to take two of our number with them to show them the way."

One by one the chiefs rose to speak. All said very much the same thing. They spoke of the beauty of their country. And, even as they expressed their wonder at the daring of these travelers into the unknown, they warned of great dangers ahead. Then, replying to Joliet's gifts, they made a present of a sleeping mat of rushes to Fr. Marquette and Joliet. The chiefs also promised to supply the travelers with guides.

Joliet made a speech of thanks, which closed the council.

On the tenth of June, they prepared to set out again. Two Miami braves were going to lead the way in their own canoe. Fr. Marquette could not help noticing how differently they wore their hair. Each had two long locks over his ears. They did not look nearly as fierce as many other Indians had looked to Fr. Marquette. Compared to the mighty Sioux, the Miamis looked far less strong. Yet they were said to have strength greater than most of the Indians known to this country, and in games and hunting they outstripped all the others.

A great crowd of Indians walked all the way from the village of the Fire Nation to watch them set out on their voyage. They were amazed at the sight of seven white men who dared to travel into the unknown country of the Southwest. They were frightened for the safety of their visitors. Even now, many of them called out to warn of terrible dangers. But Fr. Marquette knew that one of the great differences between the Indian and the white man was that the Indian always looked on the unknown with fear, and the white man looked upon it as a challenge to his daring and his courage. The Indians on the shore had made offerings to the cross in their favor. Even those who believed in the sun god made offerings to that heathen god for their safety.

Once on their way, Fr. Marquette was grateful for the two Miami guides, for the Fox River was indeed overgrown with wild rice and other water plants. In some places the channel wound through twisting curves. In others it could scarcely be found at all.

The Fox River now began to narrow steadily. Sometimes it was overgrown with rushes. Even the Miamis slowed up or stopped to study the water before pushing on. In this way they lost time, but it could not be helped, for the Fox River sometimes broadened into swampland. There were many ponds and marshes. Once they were led deep into a swamp and had to turn around, much to the shame of the Miamis.

Slower and slower they went. The river's face changed. It no longer looked like a river but only a broad creek. Then it seemed to become an ever-narrowing brook.

And at last, on their fourth day out of the Mascouten village, they could go no farther.

The Miamis stepped to the shore from their canoe, which was in the middle of the little stream which the Fox River had become. They made signs to Fr. Marquette and Joliet that this was the place of the portage. They pointed to the west across a broad, low place which led to a little rise on which trees grew. They waited while the explorers took their canoes from the waters of the Fox River and shouldered them for the portage.

The Miamis led the way, leaving their canoe behind. The travelers and Joliet carried the ladened canoes. Fr. Marquette walked unburdened. The way led through low, swampy ground for a distance of a mile and a half. Finally they entered the belt of trees on the edge of the hill. Once on. the top of the rise, the Miamis halted.

When Fr. Marquette came up to them, he saw beyond them a broad river. It was larger at this place than the Fox River had seemed at its mouth.

One of the Miamis explained that this river was called the Wisconsin, which meant river of many islands. It emptied into the great Father of Waters.

The paddlers and Joliet took the canoes over the rise to the water's edge. Then they came back to the place where Fr. Marquette stood with the guides.

"This is a real river, Father," said Joliet, excitement in his eyes.

"It will lead us to the great river," answered Fr. Marquette. "But we will be without guides. They're going back from here. They didn't agree to go any farther with us. I think they're a little scared of the great river."

Indeed, the Miamis seemed relieved at being free to go home. They expressed their friendship and loyalty, but at the same time they did not hesitate to show their alarm about the way in which the white men were determined to go. It was the way of danger to them. They had not promised to come any farther with them. They had been to the portage before, and they knew it was safe to come this far.

They made their farewells. Then they turned and ran lightly back to where they had left their canoes.

Fr. Marquette fell to his knees and bowed his head.

The others followed his example. Together they prayed to the Blessed Virgin, asking for her help and protection. They began a new devotion and resolved to repeat it every day of their voyage.

Then they went down the rise and pushed off into the waters of the Wisconsin River.

This new river was unlike any other river on which Fr. Marquette had traveled before. In place of the rocks that made the bottom of most waterways in the North, the Wisconsin River had a bottom of sand. They found out at once that this made travel more difficult. Every little while, when they thought they were in mid-stream, they came to high sandbars over which they could not paddle their canoes. Sometimes it was possible to jump out and draw them over shallow water to deep water on the other side of the bars. But most of the time they had to paddle around the bars and find the channel again.

Yet the Wisconsin was a wide river. The water had eaten away its sandy banks, and many trees had been uprooted and lay half-hidden in the water. The travelers were constantly dodging these sunken trees. The river's channel wove from shore to shore. Sometimes it took them two miles of zigzag travel to cover one straight mile. They also had to go around many heavily wooded islands on which trees hung thick and green with vines.

The Wisconsin flowed through rolling country. In the distance, hills rose as high as three hundred and fifty feet. Nearer to shore, the country was lower. Sometimes woods reached down into the water. There were oak, walnut, birch, and basswood trees. Sometimes they came to groves of locusts, and once in a while the woods gave way to open prairie country. This looked very fertile, and Fr. Marquette thought how much it would be prized by French settlers who might come to this land. Then, in turn, prairie areas gave way to heavily wooded hills again.

Though there were few ducks to be seen, there was larger game. Deer were plentiful along the Wisconsin River. Many smaller animals showed themselves from time to time. And one day Fr. Marquette caught sight of a herd of large animals.

When the paddlers drew near these animals, he saw that they were great shaggy beasts, many of them wearing curved horns. They seemed to have humps on their backs at the base of the neck.

"Are those wild cows?" he asked Joliet in wonder.

Joliet laughed heartily. "Father, those are buffalos," he answered.

"You have seen them before?" asked Fr. Marquette.

"Never," replied Joliet. "But I've heard the Indians speak of them. I know them now that I see them. They are hunted by the Sioux. They are said to be very numerous in the country of those Indians."

Early on their second day on the strange Wisconsin River, they came out of a low range of hills to an open place. A large prairie lay on their right. Far at its western rim rose steep craggy hills. On the left bank of the river rose low, gently-rounded hills, covered with oak and birch trees. Not far down the prairie stood an Indian village of some size.

Fr. Marquette and Joliet saw the village at the same time. It was not far enough from the river's edge to make it likely that they could pass without being seen.

"We need meat," said Joliet thoughtfully. "They may have some to trade."

"Let us land," decided Fr. Marquette promptly.

The Indians had already seen them. They were crowding to the shore when the canoes turned landward. All the men in the canoes looked anxiously at the Indians for any signs of hostility. There were none. Nor were there any weapons to be seen. The Indians were very curious, and as soon as Fr. Marquette and Joliet had landed, the braves made way for them to walk to the village.

When they reached the village and the braves and chiefs had all gathered around them, Fr. Marquette spoke. He tried them in one language after another, but not until he spoke the Algonquin language did they understand him.

Fr. Marquette then learned that these Indians were known as Saukies. This was their prairie. Other bands of Sauk Indians lived to the south. They belonged to the Algonquin nation. They were excited by the visit of white men and asked what the travelers were seeking.

Fr. Marquette talked to them. He told them of

the needs of the party, and they said they were willing to trade deer meat for whatever the travelers might have to barter. Then, ever mindful of his mission, Fr. Marquette preached to them, after which Joliet laid claim to the land for New France.

All the Indians crowded to the shore to see them off once more. They stood watching the two canoes move away for as long as the travelers were in sight.

Soon now the stream widened. More and more islands began to appear. They passed two more prairie areas. They went by three large swamps.

Then the hills closed in again. This time they were higher than most of the other hills the travelers had passed. At the same time, the islands became so numerous that they began to have difficulty in finding the channel of the Wisconsin River.

These signs showed that the Wisconsin was broadening toward its mouth.

6

On the Great River

DURING THEIR FOURTH day on the Wisconsin River, they approached a barrier of high hills. Indeed, a great ridge lay like a chain across their path, looming ever closer. Seen from a distance, there seemed to be no opening among them.

They went on quite uncertainly. The inlets, ponds, marshes, and islands made it almost impossible to tell what lay ahead in this wide stream, which flowed very slowly.

Suddenly Fr. Marquette found himself looking

across a broad current of water which flowed counter to the water of the Wisconsin. Beyond it rose steeply the chain of hills they had seen from a distance.

He gave a loud shout. "The great river!" he cried.

No one doubted him. In a few moments, they moved out into the wild water of the great river which swiftly absorbed the water of the Wisconsin. It flowed to the south, as the great river was said to flow.

It was the seventeenth of June, just a month since they had set out.

Fr. Marquette was glowing with joy as he looked upon the great river. He prayed to the Blessed Virgin, thanking her for helping him complete his mission and begging for her further protection. For, having reached the great river, their next task was to travel down its course to learn where it emptied. Their hope was to find an outlet to the ocean of the West.

Fr. Marquette tried to see everything about this great river at once. He had heard so much about it over so many years. Now at last he rode upon it. This Mississippi was indeed as wide as the St. Lawrence River in many places. It flowed steadily and did not rush along. It had the majesty of a large body of water moving in the knowledge that nothing could stop its flow. When they sounded the river, they found it to be very deep.

In this great river the islands and the various channels made little difference. No matter which channel they took, it led back to the main stream. All the channels carried them equally surely into the south. On the shores were many deer and buffalos. On the surface of the water fed ducks, geese, and swans by the thousands.

The waters of the Mississippi River teemed with fish. One of them struck Fr. Marquette's canoe with such force that they thought at first they had run into a fallen tree. But then they saw the fish itself—a monster which had horns at the sides of its ugly, wide mouth. It was a great gray fish with whiskers like a cat and small, wide-set eyes. But for all the fierceness of its appearance, it did not seem to have teeth.

They had scarcely recovered from the shock of being struck by this fish when one of the travelers raised a shout and pointed with his paddle. All looked in that direction and saw yet another wild creature. It was swimming across the river. It looked like a great cat. Fr. Marquette had never before seen such a large animal in the shape of a cat. They were alarmed at its appearance, but it paid no attention to them.

When they had become used to the large fish which were common in the Mississippi, they put down a net to catch some of the smaller fish so that they might have fresh fish for their next meal. The paddlers were eager to get to shore so that they could shoot one of the great buffalos. In one place, they had seen a flock of at least four hundred of the animals.

By evening, they had begun to leave the region of the high hills and had passed a few stretches of prairie. They landed at last, and some of the men went to kill a buffalo so that they might have the meat for the next few days. The others built a small campfire, only large enough to cook a meal.

None of them had any way of knowing whether unfriendly Indians were living along these strange shores.

As night deepened, they moved far away from the site of the camp before going to sleep, because an Indian who stumbled upon the remains of the buffalo might be led to the campfire's remains, and then in turn to them. They dared not risk being slain in their sleep. So they took their canoes out into the river and anchored them as far from shore as possible without getting into the main current. There they slept, crouched in the canoes, however uncomfortable it was. Even so, the men took turns on guard, so that no enemy could surprise them while they slept.

They had to accept the discomfort without complaint, for they would now have to sleep in this manner night after night.

On their eighth day on the Mississippi, while they moved along the west shore of the river, they caught sight of what appeared to be a trail leading away from the river's edge. They moved in closer to land. Other trails they had seen had proved to be those of deer or buffalos.

But this one was certainly made by men.

Fr. Marquette and Joliet beached their canoe. They got out and studied the trail. At the water's edge where the ground was soft, they could see prints of bare feet and also of moccasins. The trail was surely that of Indians. They followed it for a little way inland. It led through the trees there toward a prairie beyond.

Porteret, leader of the paddlers, called them back softly.

"You must not go along this trail, Mon Père," he cried when they came to the river again. "Nobody knows what kind of Indians made it. Besides, we have found the great river."

Fr. Marquette shook his head. "My good Porteret, we have more to do than just to find a river. I have been sent by the grace of God to convert such Indians as we find. Are we then to run in terror at the first sight of an Indian footprint?"

"The wise man does not fly into the face of danger," protested Porteret.

"There is nothing to fear," continued Fr. Marquette. "I shall make myself understood by the Indians. I shall go alone."

"No, Father. I go too," put in Joliet.

"Very well, the two of us will go. The rest remain here. If we are not back by nightfall, you must turn and go back to Quebec with our records. Do not let yourselves be surprised here. Be on guard. But do not bring on trouble either."

The five men protested, but Fr. Marquette and Joliet had made up their minds to go in along the trail. When they saw that their protests were in vain, the paddlers knelt for Fr. Marquette's blessing. They looked at him as if this might be the last time they would ever see him.

Fr. Marquette and Joliet struck into the woods. Soon they were out on a high prairie. Though they could see for some distance, there was no sign of any Indian settlement. Gnats hovered in the warm sunlight and flew into their eyes. Snakes slithered out of the way. Unknown birds cried out against them, and chipmunks made their whistling cries of alarm at sight of them.

They went on through the grass which was often shoulder-high. They knew that if hostile Indians lurked in this tall grass, they would have little chance to escape.

Suddenly, rounding a bend, they saw before them a village of Indians. It stood on the bank of a small river which flowed to the south. This river emptied into the great river at a point below the place where they had seen the trail. Beyond the village, on the slope of a hill, were two more Indian settlements.

"Do we go on?" asked Joliet.

"Yes, with God's grace," answered Fr. Marquette.

They walked steadily onward. They expected savages to come leaping out at them. But nothing stirred. They got so close to the village that they could hear the Indians talking. Then Joliet stopped.

"We'd better announce ourselves, Father," he said.

Fr. Marquette agreed.

They shouted together, making as much noise as they could. Then they stood, waiting to be seen.

They did not think it wise to walk boldly into the village lest the Indians take fright and harm them before they learned that they came as friends.

The effect of their shout was immediate. The Indians all poured out of their lodges and stood gazing at them. Fr. Marquette saw something that reassured him—some of the Indians wore woven cloth. That must mean that somewhere they had met traders. They might even be familiar with his cassock.

The Indians chattered excitedly among themselves until one of their leaders came forward toward the two travelers. It was plain to Fr. Marquette and Joliet that the Indians were on the watch for other white men. But, seeing none, they picked four older Indians, gave something to them, and pushed them forward to greet their white visitors.

The four Indians came forward cautiously. As they walked toward them, Fr. Marquette noticed that two of them carried long-stemmed pipes. These pipes were held aloft, high over their heads.

They were decorated with colored feathers and carvings. The Indians who carried them raised the pipes up and down toward the sun, as if they were offering the pipes to the sun to smoke.

But none of the Indians said a word. They came on slowly. Finally they paused and stood looking carefully at the two Frenchmen, as if they expected to be attacked at any moment.

Fr. Marquette waited no longer. He spoke to them in the Algonquin language and asked them who they were.

They answered, "We are Illinois."

Fr. Marquette was overjoyed. This then, must be the place of the Illinois to which he had been invited when he was still at La Pointe! It was where those first Illinois hunters had said it was—far to the south and west of La Pointe.

The welcoming Indians now offered them the pipes to smoke. These were pipes of peace, they explained. They were called calumets. Fr. Marquette and Joliet each took a few puffs, though the tobacco in them was very strong and made their tongues smart.

As soon as the Illinois saw that the priest and the explorer had smoked the calumets, they invited them to enter the village. They led them to a lodge where they were to be officially welcomed. There, in the doorway, stood another Illinois, with his arms and hands stretched up toward the sun. As they came up, he spoke and said, "How beautiful is the sun when you come to visit us. All our village awaits you, and you shall enter all our lodges in peace."

Then he stepped aside. Fr. Marquette and Joliet entered. The lodge was filled with braves and squaws. All watched the two white men, to see what they would do. Sometimes one of them spoke in his language, making a polite speech of welcome. Once again pipes were offered to the travelers. After they had smoked them, all the braves took a turn at the pipes.

Hardly had this been done when an Indian runner appeared at the entrance and announced in a loud voice that Chief Big Thunder of the Illinois tribes wished to hold council with the visitors. Fr. Marquette and Joliet were to follow him. Then he started away, waiting only a moment to be sure they were coming.

The Illinois were so amazed at these white men who could speak their language that they followed in a great crowd. They lined the path. Some of them lay in the grass to look at Fr. Marquette and Joliet as they passed. There were braves, squaws, old men and women, even children. Indeed, everyone from the first village was following them to the second. And all showed the two visitors great respect by making no noise to disturb them.

Big Thunder stood at the entrance to his lodge. Beside him were two old Indians who were his councilors. Like their welcomers in the first village, the chief held his calumet toward the sun as they came up.

"We wish our white friends well," he said. "We are happy to see them here in our village. We hope they will be among us for many months."

Then he offered them the calumet. Once again they had to puff at it. Fr. Marquette's tongue still burned from the last time he had smoked it. But he knew it would insult the chief if he did not smoke it.

Other chieftains had gathered inside the lodge of Big Thunder. Seeing them, Fr. Marquette thought it was now time that he too spoke to tell them how happy he was to be among them. He turned to Joliet and took from him a small roll of cloth, much prized by the Indians. Joliet had carried this and a few other trifles in case they needed to offer gifts.

Fr. Marquette gave this cloth to the chief. As he did so, he made a little speech in the Illinois language. He said that he and his friends were traveling in peace to visit all the Indian nations which lived on the great river.

Then he gave Big Thunder a long string of red and yellow beads, and he spoke again. This time he said, "The Great Spirit, who is your creator and who lives in the sky, has taken pity on you because you do not know Him. He now wishes you to know Him, and He has sent me to tell you of Him. We have seen that you worship the sun. But the sun is only one of God's creations, not God

Himself. You must all now believe in and obey the one and only God."

Then Joliet gave the chief two other gifts and told the Illinois of the might and power of the great French Governor, Count de Frontenac, who had subdued even the Iroquois. He had brought peace to all places. This governor wished the Illinois to knew that they must bring their troubles to him and not make war on other tribes. Joliet told them also that he wished to know all the Illinois knew about the great river, the sea into which it flowed, and the tribes which lived on its banks.

After he had finished, Big Thunder rose. He called forward an Indian boy who was his slave. He rested one hand on the boy's head and spoke very seriously.

"I thank you, Black Robe, and you, Frenchman, because you have visited us. The earth has never been so beautiful. The sun has never been so bright as today. Our river has never been so calm or so free of rocks. Our tobacco has never tasted so good, and our corn has never looked so well as now. We beg you to take pity on us and on our nation. You know the Great Spirit who has made us all. You speak to Him. You hear His word. Beg Him to give us life and health. And you stay and live with us so that we may come to know the Great Spirit of whom you speak."

Then he offered the slave to Fr. Marquette, but Fr. Marquette quickly rose and spoke. He thanked Big Thunder but said that he could not accept the slave. All men were equal before God who had created them all. None could be a slave. He knew that Big Thunder did him great honor, but he could not accept this gift.

Big Thunder was surprised. He next offered the boy to Joliet. His name, he said, was Little Fox. He would be helpful and faithful.

Joliet thanked him and accepted Little Fox.

Big Thunder then brought forward another gift for Fr. Marquette. This was a calumet. It was a kind of pipe made of red stone, which was highly polished. The stone had been bored so that one end served as a bowl for tobacco, while the other fitted into a stem. The stem was of wood and was two feet long. It was as big as a walking stick and was bored through the middle. The stem was decorated with the heads and necks of many colorful birds. Feathers of red, green, blue, and yellow were also attached to it.

As he handed this gift to Fr. Marquette, Big Thunder made another speech. He said he had great respect for the French Governor. If all Fr. Marquette and Joliet had said of him were true, then indeed he must be a great man. Then Big Thunder's face grew very serious.

"But we beg you, on behalf of the Illinois nation, to go no farther," he said. "You will meet great dangers. There are savage Indians who live on the banks of the Father of Waters. There are monsters who live in its depths. All are anxious to kill travelers. Do not go."

"I do not fear death," answered Fr. Marquette as he thanked Chief Big Thunder. "There is no joy greater for me than to lose my life for the glory of Him who has created us all."

The Illinois were astonished at this speech. They could not understand how a man could think so little of his life. They decided that Fr. Marquette's

God must indeed be great to inspire such faith.

Now the chief announced that there would be a great feast and entertainment in honor of the visitors. The Illinois had begun to make ready for this as soon as they saw that Fr. Marquette and Joliet were friendly.

But Fr. Marquette would not sit down to eat until someone went back to the river to tell Porteret and the others that the Indians were friendly. Otherwise, the travelers might think that Fr. Marquette and Joliet had been killed, and they might leave without them. Joliet himself went back. Not until he returned did Big Thunder give the signal for the feast to begin.

One of the Indians, who was in charge of the feast, seated Fr. Marquette and Joliet. Then he served them. Neither was allowed to help himself. The Illinois considered it a mark of respect to feed their guests themselves.

First Fr. Marquette and Joliet were fed sagamité. This was a dish of Indian corn meal, boiled and flavored with fat. The Indian in charge filled spoons full of sagamité and put the food into the mouths of his guests. Next he fed them baked fish. He broke off pieces of the fish with his fingers, blew on them to cool them, removed the bones, and put them into the mouths of Fr. Marquette and Joliet. Then came a dish of which neither could eat. This was roasted dog. The Illinois had killed the dog especially for them. When Big Thunder saw that they would not eat this meat, he made a sign for it to be taken away. Then, for the last course, they were fed pieces of wild ox.

All this fatty food came close to making Fr. Marquette ill. Yet he did not show that the food was unpleasant for him. This would have insulted the Illinois. They might then have thought less of him, and they might in turn refuse to accept the word of God.

As soon as the guests had been fed, the entertainment began. This took the form of a calumet dance. It was performed in an open place surrounded by trees. The Illinois ringed this place, sitting in the shade of the trees. In the middle of the open place, a large, brightly painted mat of rushes was put down. As Fr. Marquette and Joliet came up with the chief, the figure of a bird was carried out and put upon the mat.

"That is the Manitou of the dancer," explained Big Thunder. "It is his sign of good luck. Whoever among us dreams of a bird or a snake or a fish takes it for his Manitou. His success in war or in the hunt is given him by his Manitou."

The peace calumet was placed next to the bird figure. Other Indians came forward and placed before the calumet war-clubs, hatchets, arrows, quivers, bracelets, bows, and head-bands which they had won in battles. This was to show their respect for the peace calumet. Then those who were to sing took their place under the trees. Each, as he came, saluted the Manitou by breathing in smoke from the calumet and blowing it on the Manitou.

The dance was begun as soon as the singers were in their places. First a number of braves, one at a time, took the calumet and danced with it while the singers chanted. Then the formal beginner of the dance made his appearance. He continued where the other dancers had left off. He took the calumet and offered it to the sun. Then he bent it toward the earth. After this, he pretended that it could fly. Finally, he carried it around, dancing all the while, and offered it to the watchers so that they could take puffs. All this was done in perfect timing with the music of a drum and a gourd.

When this was finished, he made a sign to a brave and invited him to come into the circle and fight with him. The brave who was invited stepped in and took up one of the weapons which had been laid before the calumet. Then the two of them danced around in mock battle. First the brave would pretend to strike at the dancer; then the dancer would fend off his blows with his calumet. In the end, the calumet bearer won, because, according to the Illinois, the calumet was all powerful. He pranced all about, holding the calumet high, and Big Thunder, to signify the end of the dance, presented a buffalo robe to him.

The day was now drawing to a close. Yet Big Thunder invited Fr. Marquette and Joliet to visit the whole village. This meant that they had to walk to each of the three hundred Indian lodges. Tired though they were, they did not refuse, but accepted Big Thunder's invitation with thanks.

When they set out, an Illinois went before them, shouting in a loud voice. He commanded all the Illinois to come from their lodges and see the visitors. He forbade them to annoy the travelers in any way.

Before they had completed their visits, darkness had fallen, and the bonfires had been lit. The Indian dogs, which abounded in the camp, came back into the streets from which they had been chased before.

Fr. Marquette and Joliet were led to Big Thunder's lodge. This had been made ready for them. Here they would stay for the few days they intended to visit the Illinois. There Big Thunder made his formal farewell and left them to sleep.

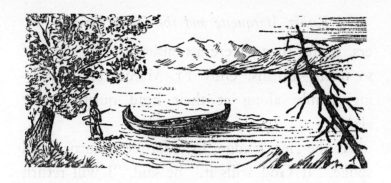

7

Down the Mississippi

ON THE MORNING when they left the Illinois, Big Thunder himself led his visitors back the way they had come. All the way he was warning them. He told them again of the dangers to the south. He told them to make good use of the calumet. He said they must turn back at the slightest sign of hostility. He told them most seriously that the Indians who lived to the south were savages.

Over six hundred of the Illinois followed. When they came in sight of the river, the waiting travelers, seeing them, were astonished at the sight of so many Indians. Only Fr. Marquette's marching calmly along at their head quieted their alarm.

At the river's edge, Fr. Marquette turned and spoke. "If God wills it," he said, "I will return within a year and teach you about Him."

So many of the Indians made speeches in reply, that it was afternoon before the two canoes pushed out from shore. Even then the Illinois were not willing to see them go. No Indians had ever showed themselves so happy to see visitors. None had ever before so urgently begged Fr. Marquette to teach them of the God whose children were both white and red.

Soon after leaving the Illinois, the canoes drove in along a rocky bank which was both high and long. Much to their astonishment, Fr. Marquette and Joliet saw that some savage artist had painted great beasts upon the rocks. There were two of them, both painted in green, red, and black. They were horned beasts with red eyes and beards. Though in the shape of four-legged animals, they had human faces. Their bodies were scaled, and they had long tails that wound about their bodies. Fr. Marquette had never seen such monsters.

"Can it be there are such beasts as these?" he asked Joliet, remembering how many of the Indians had warned them to beware of monsters.

"I doubt it, Father," answered Joliet. "Else one of us would surely have seen something of them before this."

The quiet, deep water moved steadily southward. Soon they were carried past the painted rocks, though Fr. Marquette kept his eyes on them long enough to make drawings of the two monsters in his records.

Now from ahead of them came a great roaring. This sound became louder as they went down river. Joliet guessed that they were nearing some rapids. But the sound grew to such volume as they neared it that Joliet next thought it was a waterfall.

Yet it was neither of these. Even as they began shouting from one canoe to the other, telling each other to move toward shore and prepare to portage, they came in sight of the source of the rushing waters which made the noise.

The roaring of the waters was made by the meeting of the Mississippi with another great river. This stream came in out of the northwest. At its mouth, it was as broad as the Mississippi. In its waters churned whole trees, many large branches, and floating islands of sticks and leaves which had been collected in the violent currents. The water which came into the Mississippi at this point was very muddy. Fr. Marquette immediately named the new river the Pekitanoui, which meant muddy water.

The Illinois had told them of this river. They had said it flowed down to the Mississippi past great prairies, which stretched for many, many miles without being broken even by a hill. It flowed past many Indian villages. Its water was always brown. Fr. Marquette would like to have gone up this river, but their course lay to the south.

The waters which joined here were so choppy that they had all they could do to pass in safety. Their light, little canoes spun like corks. The paddlers had to dodge great trees as well as swirling branches which often bobbed up from beneath. They had to turn the canoes this way and that, tossed about by the violent waters. They were not out of danger for a moment while they passed the mouth of the great muddy river. For some time after they had gone by, they continued to find themselves among floating trees.

But at length they reached a quieter stretch of water. Yet even here the muddy water of the northwest river was to be seen; it had colored the Mississippi for miles around.

Soon after, they camped for the night. As usual, Fr. Marquette wandered into the woods and open lands that were nearby. There were no dwellings in sight. But he found and marveled at honeysuckle and cactus in blossom. He came upon mulberry trees on which the fruit was ripening, and he picked many berries to take back to camp.

He did not stay long away from the canoes, however. For now, with every lap farther south that they made, they met more and more of a kind of pest they had not seen many of in the North.

These were mosquitoes. They made each camp so miserable with their attacks that all were glad to be in the boats. Sometimes the mosquitoes did not find them there. Or, if they did, the men rigged up canvas tent covers under which they could all sleep. When they were moving, the mosquitoes did not very often bother them.

Thus far, no one had seen anything of the monsters of whom the various tribes had warned Fr. Marquette and Joliet. But on the third day after they had passed the mouth of the big muddy river, they neared a similar roaring sound. This, according to the Illinois, was the home of the demon who swallowed men and canoes alike.

But this was less frightening than the mouth of the muddy river, for the canoes did not have to go through it. It was a deep, narrow gorge, close to one shore of the river. It was walled in by tall rocks which reared up twenty feet from the water's surface. Between them, the water forced its way. It was flung first against one wall and then against the next. This made not only a great noise but also a churning foam. It was no wonder, thought Fr.

Marquette, that this demon swallowed men and canoes. If any traveler were foolish enough to drive his canoe into those leaping waters, both would be lost. The Illinois had told Fr. Marquette during his visit with them that a great being of evil dwelled under these churning waters and seized all who went by.

Beyond the gorge, the water of the Mississippi was soon quiet once more.

Fr. Marquette was always scanning the shores for signs of Indian villages. He saw none. But he was not surprised to find so few settlements. He had learned long ago that Indians had no judgment of distance. If an Indian said that there was another village only a few days' journey away, it was likely to take ten or twelve days to reach it.

He busied himself whenever he could with making notes about the places where there might be iron deposits and about the clay banks which gave the Indians their dyes. Their color held so well that when Fr. Marquette dipped his paddle into the clay at one place, the color stayed on it many days.

On the eighth day after they had left the Illinois tribes, they sighted other Indians. Porteret saw them first. He gave a shout and pointed toward shore. Twenty braves lined the shore. At once Joliet gave the signal for a careful approach.

The Indians were unlike any Fr. Marquette had seen. As the canoes came close, some of the men pulled up their paddles and took up their guns instead. Fr. Marquette saw that the braves wore their hair long and tattooed their bodies as the Iroquois did. Yet he was sure that these Indians were not Iroquois. They were too far south of Iroquois country.

Fr. Marquette stood up carefully in the canoe. The Indians were beckoning them to come closer. He held aloft the calumet and called out words of greeting in the Huron language.

One of the Indians answered at once. As nearly as he could understand what he heard, Fr. Marquette thought the reply was a declaration of war. He almost faltered. But, since no one on shore made a warlike move, he decided that he had made a mistake in what he thought the Indian had said.

"Do you know these Indians?" he asked Joliet.

"I've never seen their like before," answered Joliet. "They don't fire on us, though. They must be Chickasaws. Didn't the Illinois say they would be the next ones?"

"Let us go in, then," said Fr. Marquette.

The two canoes made for shore, though the paddlers muttered aloud at the danger they ran. As they came close, they heard the Indian speaker once more. This time Fr. Marquette was relieved to understand his broken Huron speech perfectly. The travelers were only being invited to land and share the Indians' food!

There was a small Chickasaw settlement just beyond some bushes which lined the shore at that place. It consisted of but a single row of lodges. The five men who had landed were invited to enter one of the lodges. Two paddlers had to remain behind with the canoes to guard them.

Fr. Marquette did not hesitate even though Porteret grumbled warningly. His confidence was not misplaced. Inside, the neatly dressed Chickasaw squaws had spread a small meal of dried buffalo meat, which had been softened with bear's grease, and some wild white plums.

After they had finished eating, Fr. Marquette offered the braves in the lodge some of his medals. They took them with delight and thanked him not in their own language, but in the imperfect Huron they had heard him speak.

All the time, Fr. Marquette was using his eyes to learn all he could about this tribe. He saw that these Indians were no strangers to white men, for they owned cloth, guns, knives, beads, and glass powder flasks. He asked them how far they were from the sea into which the great river emptied.

The oldest among them answered, "Ten days' journey."

"That means at least twenty," said Joliet aside.

"Where have you seen other white men?" asked Fr. Marquette.

The old Indian pointed to the east. He spoke slowly, feeling his way in the Huron language. He said they bought cloth and other goods from the white traders to the east. He told Fr. Marquette that there were Black Robes there, too. They had rosaries and holy pictures and also medals. They were kind to the Indians, and the Chickasaws had been kind to them in turn.

Fr. Marquette then made a short speech in which he told them about God. There were no converts among them. Yet all listened to him with respect, though he was not sure that they knew enough of the Huron language to have understood him.

The old Indian, who was the spokesman of the little settlement, thanked him. Then he said what Fr. Marquette and his friends had come to expect they would hear. He warned them not to go much farther down the Mississippi River. He said that farther south there were savages and other great dangers to travelers.

Then the Chickasaws led them back to the place where they had left their canoes and watched them swing out again into the great river. The Indians stood watching them for as long as the canoes were in sight.

But they were not in sight for long, for they were now past the region of prairies and traveled between walls of forest trees. These giant trees stood very high and rose on great round trunks, sometimes hung with vines. Though they saw no more buffalos, they still heard them bellowing beyond the trees. Along the river, ducks and geese had given place to quail and beautifully colored birds—red, green, and yellow. These were paroquets. They were of the same size as the mourning dove, and they filled the air with the sound of their voices.

They went through this peaceful country for several days without seeing a dwelling of any kind. The men hoped soon to come to the end of the river. None of them liked the hot weather of this country, so far from the northern lakes and rivers to which they were accustomed.

Then, one day, Joliet's Indian boy, Little Fox, spoke urgently to them. "Listen," he said.

"Blue jays," said Fr. Marquette.

Little Fox nodded his head quickly. "Yes, the jays cry out. The other birds are still. Someone is near in the woods."

Fr. Marquette translated this for Joliet, who was

alert at once. "That's true," he said. He began to look around.

Suddenly, fearful shouts and yells rang out. Looking shoreward, they saw a large crowd of painted Indians bursting from the woods. Some of them carried war clubs. Some waved hatchets and shields. Some had bows and arrows. Indeed, even as the travelers looked at them, they saw arrows come hurtling in their direction.

Once more the paddlers reached for their guns. Canoes were being pushed out from shore by the Indians. Some were heading south to cut them off from that direction. Some drove north so that the canoes of the white travelers could not retreat.

"Do not fire," said Joliet firmly.

"Blessed Virgin, grant us your protection," prayed Fr. Marquette.

He took hold of the peace calumet of the Illinois and stood up in the canoe. He raised the calumet high so that the Indians could see it.

No one made a move.

Joliet said, "They're trying to scare us off. They're afraid of us."

"We have guns. They don't," said Porteret.

"There are too many of them. We don't dare fire on them. They can kill us all, no matter how many of them we shoot," answered Joliet.

A war club came flying past, narrowly missing Fr. Marquette's head. Yet he did not flinch. He continued to stand calmly there. On his face was a broad smile.

On the shore, some of the young braves ran down to the water's edge and threw themselves in. They were trying to swim out and attack the canoes. But the current forced them back. It was now clear to the travelers that an Indian village lay just behind this place on the shore, for it was to and from it that the Indians were moving.

Fr. Marquette tried to make signs to show that they were friendly. But the Indians did not seem to understand. It began to look as if at any moment a shower of arrows would be loosed upon them.

"Let us go a little closer," said Fr. Marquette suddenly. "I don't believe they see the calumet."

"They might not know what it is," said Porteret warningly.

Nevertheless, they moved slowly in toward shore.

Now Fr. Marquette could plainly see, well down along the shore, at the very edge of the water, a group of old men. These older Indians were beginning to restrain the young braves. Fr. Marquette continued to stand in the canoe with the calumet held high above his head. He could not be sure that his frail body would not be pierced by a hatchet or an arrow at any moment, but he was certain that his prayer for protection would be heard.

The cries and yells died down. Arrows and war clubs stopped flying at them. The Indians stood there watching them come in.

Finally, the canoes touched the shore.

At once two of the old men leaped into the canoe nearest them and made signs to invite them all to their village.

Fr. Marquette tried them with all the six languages he knew. He tried them with the language of the Illinois. But only one old man among them could speak the Illinois language, and he alone knew what Fr. Marquette was trying to say. He struggled for the attention of the others, but they were so excited that it took a while until he could be heard.

Then he cried out, "They come in peace. They bring presents. They wish to hold council with us."

From him, Fr. Marquette and Joliet learned that they had come to the village of the Mitchegameas.

8

Faces North

THE MITCHEGAMEAS were so relieved that the white men were friendly that they treated them like royal visitors. Yet, the Indians did not put away their warlike attitudes. This troubled Fr. Marquette a little, but he tried not to show it. It worried Joliet, too.

Still, they could not refuse the hospitality of the Mitchegameas. They were invited to eat and were given sagamité and fish. Then they were told that Chief Banded Snake wished them to be his guests for the night and to rest themselves well.

Fr. Marquette thanked him and accepted this invitation too, though he would have preferred to go on. Yet he could not pass over any chance to preach to the savages, especially to those who, like these Indians, had had few contacts with white men. It did not appear that the Mitchegameas had even met traders, for there did not seem to be a gun in the village. And Indians, whenever they began to trade with white men, always wanted to own the thunder-sticks of the traders. But because he had to preach in the language of the Illinois, he could not be sure that they knew what he said to them.

Joliet had little better success when it came to questions he asked about the great river and the sea into which it flowed. Either the Mitchegameas did not know how to answer or they did not wish to. They said only that the travelers would find the answers to their questions in the next village, which was not far down the river. The Indians who lived there belonged to the Arkansas nation. They were closer to the sea, so they would know more about it.

Banded Snake promised that he would send word to the Arkansas, and in the morning when they set out, he would send a canoe full of his warriors to guide the party to the next village.

"This I promise you," he said solemnly. "A Mitchegamea does not tell untruths."

They spent a restless night. They were uneasy because of the warlike attitude of these Indians. But they need not have worried. Banded Snake kept his word. When they reached the river's edge next morning, they found there one of the Mitchegamea's large, crude, but strong canoes, together with ten Indians ready to lead the way.

As usual, everyone in the village saw them off. All the Mitchegameas crowded along the shore. They shouted their good wishes to the travelers. Some of them shouted warnings of the dangers which were in store for them. They were like all the other Indians—afraid of what they did not know.

The Mitchegameas in the lead canoe paddled with great vigor, just as if they were showing off how strong they were. The travelers had all they could do just to keep up.

Fortunately, they did not have far to go. The village of the Arkansas was only a few hours away from that of the Mitchegameas.

They were not yet within sight of the Arkansas village when they met two canoes. They were filled with Arkansas, who had been sent out to meet them. Banded Snake, true to his promise, had sent word of their coming. Now the Arkansas were prepared to receive the white men in friendship.

The leader of the Indians in the canoes stood upright. He held up the calumet. None of the Arkansas appeared hostile.

As the canoes neared one another, the paddlers began to slow down so that they might come together gently. The leading canoe of the Arkansas came up alongside that in which Fr. Marquette and Joliet sat. The Indian in command turned to them and made signs of welcome while the Arkansas braves and the white paddlers held the canoes together in the strong current. He often used the calumet to make motions. When he had finished, he offered the calumet for Joliet and Fr. Marquette to smoke.

After the white men had puffed at the pipe of peace, the Arkansas offered them sagamité. Both Joliet and Fr. Marquette made signs to say that they had eaten not long before with the Mitchegameas. Nothing daunted, the Arkansas leader gave each of them little cakes baked of corn meal. On these the travelers nibbled politely. They found them quite good. The leader surprised them by singing gently while they ate the little cakes.

Satisfied now, the Arkansas leader told them to follow. The Indians let go of the canoe and pushed themselves ahead of the lighter canoes of their visitors. At the same time, the heavy canoe of the Mitchegameas swung around and, with much shouting of farewells from the Indians, turned back.

The canoe of the Arkansas now led the way to the Arkansas village. This was just around a bend. They saw it at once, for all the Arkansas were on the shore, waiting for them. A way had been left for them to walk in among the lodges to the dwelling of the chief.

The chief of the Arkansas was named Two Smokes. He stood holding the calumet to welcome them. Before him, new, clean rush mats had been placed for the white visitors. The other Indians sat in circles around Two Smokes. The old braves sat closest. Then came a circle of young warriors. In the outer ring were as many squaws and children as could find room. Behind Fr. Marquette and Joliet, the circle closed when the Indians who had brought them from the Mississippi River to the village followed them into the chief's lodge.

A young Indian brave stepped forward to stand at the side of Two Smokes. He began to talk to Fr. Marquette and Joliet in the Illinois language. He explained that the chieftain of the Mitchegameas had sent word that their white visitors could speak only the Illinois language and that he had learned this speech when he had been among the Illinois two summers gone by. Now he would interpret the speech between the white men and Two Smokes.

While the young brave spoke, Fr. Marquette looked around him. Unlike many Indians he had seen, these Arkansas wore their hair short. Their ears and noses had been pierced and were hung with beads. Yet the women wore no ornaments, and hardly enough skins to cover them. The men wore only loin cloths. It was plain to Fr. Marquette that the Arkansas were very poor Indians. They did not own guns. They did not have enough ornaments for their women. Their only riches were in the many hills of corn which stood high all around the village.

When Two Smokes had finished making his greeting, Fr. Marquette rose and spoke. Once more he talked of the glory of God, their God and his own, though they had not known of Him until now. Once again he spoke of the Governor of New France, and said that they were his people and were under his protection. He told the Arkansas, as he had told the tribes before them, that he had been sent to teach them about God.

Two Smokes made a thoughtful answer through his interpreter. "What the Black Robe has said is pleasing to my spirit. We would like to hear more of the Great Manitou of the white men. Perhaps the Black Robe will stay and teach us more of Him?"

Fr. Marquette replied that he was sorry, but he could not stay. Perhaps some day he would come back to live among them. Or another like him would come.

"Where does the Black Robe hope to go now?" asked Two Smokes.

"We seek the mouth of the great river. We wish to learn of the sea into which it empties. Then we must return to the north from whence we came," said Fr. Marquette. "Can you tell us how far away the sea is? And of the way to it?"

Two Smokes nodded his head with a serious look on his bronze face. "I say to my brother, the Black Robe—do not go. The sea is but ten days' journey. In the light boats of the white men, perhaps it is but five days away. The great river empties into the great bay. The sun at noon burns like fire straight ahead. Beyond the bay is the sea."

If Fr. Marquette had had any doubt before, now

he was sure that the Mississippi emptied not into the western sea but into the Gulf of Mexico. He had begun to think this many days ago.

Two Smokes went on. "With every hour on the great river to the south, you ride into ever greater danger. There are many unfriendly tribes on both shores of the great river. There are the Chickasaw and the Choctaw and the Natchez and the Atakapa. All have guns. They have traded with white men who speak a different language."

That would be the Spanish, thought Fr. Marquette.

"White men and our red brothers along the great river will fire upon strangers without warning. They have kept us poor. Look about you. Do you see guns? Do you see beads? Do you see anything but the poorest things? No. That is because the unfriendly tribes surround us. We are not allowed to trade with white men. We are forced to part with our buffalo hides in exchange for knives, hatchets, and a few beads. We dare not go down the great river. We dare not go far from our village to hunt the wild cattle. Our enemies are strong and well armed. We are weak and poorly armed. They have kept us so. We dare not anger such strong enemies. We say to you—do not go. You will never reach the sea."

This was the same thing that other Indians had told Fr. Marquette and Joliet. Yet this time Fr. Marquette was inclined to believe what he heard. Two Smokes had done what other Indians had not. He had offered proof that he spoke the truth. Indeed, it was hard to believe that any Indians would willingly remain so poor and so defenseless if they were not forced to do so.

Two Smokes did not wait for Fr. Marquette to speak again. He gave a signal to Indians who waited at the entrance of his lodge. Almost immediately food was brought and put down before the guests. All the Indians present were allowed to scramble for some of it. This they did in an orderly manner. Nevertheless, they showed how hungry they were.

The food was the customary sagamité, followed by great platters of dog meat. But there was something more which Fr. Marquette and Joliet ate with great enjoyment. This was corn, roasted on the ears. Then, as an added treat, the Arkansas served watermelons which they had grown among their corn hills.

While they ate, Two Smokes told them about his tribe. He said that the Arkansas were not of the tribes to the north. They did not belong to the Algonquin nation, nor yet to the mighty Sioux nation. They had come up far from the Southwest. They were descended from the great Aztec nation. They had come to the great river by way of the Colorado River and the river of the Arkansas, which emptied into the Father of Waters from the west not far away. They had suffered many misfortunes, and their pride had been humbled.

For all the rest of that day, food was served to the Arkansas and their guests. The occasion was one of great celebration. But several times Fr. Marquette noticed that envious eyes were cast upon their clothes and upon the little store of gifts that remained after they had given clasp-knives, cloth, and holy pictures to Two Smokes. He felt uneasy and was happy when at last they were taken to a small bark-covered lodge where they would spend the night.

It was not yet dawn when Little Fox woke Fr. Marquette and Joliet. He made signs to command their silence. Then he whispered that several times in the night someone had come to look in upon them.

"We must leave this place," he said earnestly. "There are Indians here who would take meat."

To take meat, Fr. Marquette knew, meant to kill.

Little Fox had hardly spoken when an Indian stepped quietly into their lodge. Then another came to stand beside the first.

"You are awake," said the interpreter's voice. "Good. Be still now. It is Two Smokes who would have speech with you."

Two Smokes began to talk in a troubled voice. "In the night some of my braves came to me. They asked me to let them slay you and divide your possessions among them. They are very poor. I have forbidden this. It is not meet that men with whom we have smoked the pipe of peace and eaten together should be treated in this manner. I come now to tell you this. I come to tell you I will protect you as long as you remain in my village."

As soon as he had finished speaking, Two Smokes solemnly danced the calumet dance for them. Then he gave them his own calumet to make sure that they believed in his promise. After this, he bade them farewell and left their lodge, followed by his interpreter.

All the men were now awake. Dawn was just beginning to show in the East. The men were already making plans to return to the canoes.

Porteret said what they were all thinking. "We do not trust these Indians."

"The only question is, do we go down the river or back up?" asked Joliet.

Fr. Marquette did not hesitate to speak his mind. "There are many thousands of poor souls there below us. How can we think of going back without bringing them to God?"

Joliet looked at him with compassion.

The other men said nothing, only went on making ready to go back to the canoes.

"Father, we know now that the great river empties into the Gulf of Mexico, not the western sea," said Joliet, shaking his head. "The great river is not the way to the western sea. We need not go on. It is now two months since we started from St. Ignatius. Even if we could return with the same speed, it would be the middle of September before we got back. But we cannot go at the same speed against the current as we came with it. Besides, Father, you have not grown stronger in the past few weeks."

Fr. Marquette knew that this was the truth. He had hoped no one had noticed it, but that hope was in vain. Even now he was not sure that he would be able to return the way they had come.

"I think only of my duty to these poor savages," he said quietly. "I cannot think of myself."

"But we have another duty too," said Joliet. "We must see to it that our records are brought safely back. We owe that much to the Governor of New France and to your Superior General, Father. There is proof at every hand that we have at last come among those unfriendly tribes of which we have been warned at every stop along the way. The proof is in the poverty of the Arkansas tribe. They are without guns, and Indians who are free to trade always have guns. And even among them, there are those who would willingly kill us if they were not held back from doing so."

Porteret nodded eagerly. "We must go back now. Else it will be too late. The ice will come."

"We have accomplished our mission, Father," Joliet went on. "We were sent to find the great river and learn its course. We have done so. We have made maps and kept records for those who will come after us. All these would be lost if we were to go on and fall into the hands of either hostile Indians or the Spanish. The former would kill us, and the latter would imprison us and seize or destroy all our records."

"But we are only ten days, perhaps less, from the sea!" said Fr. Marquette.

"That is what the Indians say. But I know better than to trust them, and so do you. They cannot measure distance. It may indeed be but ten days through hostile country; it may be twenty or even more. It is now late in the year, though the weather is still hot here. We do not know any of the languages spoken to the south. And the storms in this country are as bad as snow and ice in the North. If we go on, even if we met no Indians or Spanish, we would surely meet the storms of which the Indians speak, and then on the way back, snow and ice too. I fear we would never return."

"I never expected to be either comfortable or safe," said Fr. Marquette gently. "No one has offered me protection. No one will punish those who might take my life or my possessions."

"But you were not sent on this journey as a martyr, Father. And none of us has any right to endanger our new-found knowledge."

"That is true. But even more," said Fr. Marquette, glancing at the waiting travelers, "no one—least of all myself—has the right to put the lives of these men in any more danger than they have already faced. Nevertheless, my soul is sad. What you say is right, Louis. We are not free men here. We must turn back now."

They made their way back to the river like shadows in the gray dawn light. They went by the same path they had walked in triumph only the day before. Now they went secretly, careful to make no sound.

Their canoes had not been touched. They lay where they had been left. The men lifted them, put in their belongings, and pushed off.

With one accord, they turned north, facing back the way they had come. The day was the seventeenth of July, just a month since they had first looked upon the great river.

9

Back to St. Francis Xavier

ONE DAY IN AUGUST, they passed the place where the muddy river from the west entered the Mississippi River. Soon thereafter, they saw the mouth of another river which was emptying into the Mississippi from the east. Little Fox suddenly grew very excited. He pointed eagerly to the mouth of this river and cried out that they must go into it.

"Quick way," he kept saying. "That is the river of the Illinois. Many Illinois live on it."

Joliet paid little attention to him. They were all

very tired. For weeks they had threaded their way along the great river. They had woven among many islands and had lost their way in marshes, looking for smooth water where the violent current would not always be tugging and pulling them.

But Fr. Marquette questioned Little Fox. After all, the little Indian boy knew where they were going. Perhaps he did know a short way to Lake Michigan. They were now not far from the country of the Illinois whom they had visited on the way down the river.

"We go this way many times," said Little Fox. "The river comes from the north. Then there are two other rivers across the portage. They flow into the great lake you seek."

Fr. Marquette told Joliet what Little Fox had said.

"Very well," said Joliet. "We'll try it."

They turned and left the swift Father of Waters to push their way into the gentler Illinois River. Soon they were in a country of forests and grassy plains, a place of much game and many fish. Best of all, it was a land free at last of the mosquitoes which had made their journey north an unending misery.

During all the journey north, Joliet had watched Fr. Marquette anxiously. Though he never shirked his duty and took his place at the paddle every day, Fr. Marquette was no longer a well man. Every day his stroke seemed a little less strong. Every morning, though he had lain quiet all night, he was still pale, and he did not appear to have rested. Yet the sight of the Illinois River seemed to please him.

As they sat around their campfire that first night on the Illinois, Joliet watched Fr. Marquette write in his journal. He looked over his shoulder and read.

"We have seen nothing like this beautiful river," Fr. Marquette wrote. "Its soil is very fertile. There are many prairies and woods. There are wild cattle, elks, deer, wildcats, geese, swans, ducks, paroquets, and even some beavers."

"I had not thought to see you here again, Father," said Joliet soberly. "I have seen that you were ill."

"The good Lord has not yet wished me to die,"

answered Fr. Marquette simply. "There is work for me to do."

"We cannot hope to reach Quebec before the ice sets in," Joliet went on. "It is already late, and the nights are growing cooler."

"There will be a place for us somewhere, never fear," said Fr. Marquette.

"We still have a long way to go," Joliet reminded him. "But at least we're back in the Illinois Indian country. We should soon come to one of their villages where we can get more supplies."

But it was more than a week before they came to a village of Illinois Indians at a place known as Starved Rock. The Illinois village was named Kaskaskia. Like all the Illinois, they were very friendly. They hailed their visitors with much shouting and many expressions of pleasure. At once they took the travelers to a lodge from among the seventy-four which made up their village.

Tired and ill though he was, Fr. Marquette spent the three days of their visit going from lodge to lodge, preaching the gospel. The Illinois followed him, and Chief Blue Goose of that village himself begged Fr. Marquette to come back and live with them.

When they were ready to leave the village, Blue Goose sent one of the younger chiefs and six braves to go with them. The young chief's name was Red Feather. He explained that the Illinois thought so much of Fr. Marquette that they had sent him to guide the white men from the Illinois River to the Des Plaines River and out into Lake Michigan by way of the Chicago River.

Joliet was delighted. The Indian guides knew their country better than any of the travelers.

Just as they were ready to leave on the morning of the fourth day, a group of the Illinois beckoned to Fr. Marquette. He hurried over to them and found one of them holding a sick child.

"Make him better, Black Robe," the Indians begged him.

Fr. Marquette examined the child as much as he could. He saw readily that this boy was dying.

"I cannot. He is in God's hands," he answered them in their language. "But I will baptize him in God's name."

While they watched him with eager attention and hope in their dark eyes, Fr. Marquette baptized the dying boy.

Later, when he had rejoined Joliet in the canoe, he said, "If this voyage results only in the salvation of that one soul, then all my troubles will have been well rewarded."

"Even to your own death, Father?" asked Joliet.

"Surely to that," answered Fr. Marquette. "I am only God's most humble servant."

When they set out again, the Illinois gathered at the river and chanted a farewell song to them. Red Feather and his braves took the lead, and soon they were out of sight of the village.

They pushed on for days. Red Feather led the way straight to the Des Plaines River, and they went up that river as far as they could go. Then he headed the portage to the Chicago River. Their way led through woods and over prairies, rich in game. Here they made up for the many days along the great river when they had had very little to eat.

Finally they came out of the Chicago River. Ahead of them lay Lake Michigan, far south of that place where they had left it to go up the Fox River months before. At the shore of the lake, Red Feather and his braves bade the white men farewell.

"We go back now," he said. "Your way is clear and free before you. Ours is clear before us. We look to the time when the Black Robe can return to live among our people."

"Go with God," answered Fr. Marquette. "By His grace, I will return to be with you."

The Indians turned back. The white men, once more alone, pushed on up the western shore of the lake. They moved against a strong southward current. Their goal was the mission of St. Francis Xavier. Further than that, they could not hope to go, for it was already late September, and in the North the weather in many places was already bitter cold. The travelers had begun to feel a little of the winter cold at night.

They followed the shore as closely as they dared. After so many weeks on the rivers, they had to get used to lake travel all over again, especially in their light river canoes. They could not plan their traveling time, because the weather was so changeable. Sometimes the sun shone, the air was warm, and the breezes were gentle. After such days, they camped on the beach under the stars. But sometimes the wind blew with such force that they dared not put their canoes into the water at all. They had to move their camping sites far up away from the beach, out of reach of the huge waves. During storms, they crouched under the canoes on the mats of rushes given them by the Indians.

Day followed day. Their journey seemed endless. They never seemed to make any gain in the hundred and fifty miles they had to go to reach the long bay into which the Fox River emptied. Little Fox knew this bay by its Indian name— Sturgeon Bay.

But at last they came to the Indian portage across the peninsula of land which separated them from the waters of Sturgeon Bay. To go around the peninsula would mean more than a hundred extra miles of paddling. They had battled the rough waters of Lake Michigan for too many days to want to travel on them any more than necessary.

The paddlers were tired, too, even though their outdoor life had made them stronger than most white men. But they never complained, and they were happy to be so close to their goal. Reaching the shore, they jumped from the canoes and pulled them up out of the water. Tired as they were, they tied the baggage to their backs and shouldered the canoes.

Fr. Marquette was not allowed to carry anything, though Joliet took more than his share of the baggage. Neither of them had to help with the canoes. The paddlers could carry them more easily alone.

Pine forest lined the portage on both sides. They plunged into this forest and gulped great breaths of the pine-scented air, which seemed so fresh and perfumed after the wet spray of the lake. They were in luck, for they could carry all their supplies without making return trips for anything. Even so, they had to stop very often to rest, for they were weary after the long pull up the lake.

The portage extended for two miles. Despite many rests, it did not seem long, and at last the travelers sighted the waters of Sturgeon Bay. Now danger was left behind them. They were in country that they knew, and not far away lay their goal.

They put the canoes into the water, eager to complete their long journey.

The next day they entered the mouth of the Fox River, and in a short time they came within sight of the mission of St. Francis Xavier.

Their approach had been seen. Like all Indians living along waterways, the Winnebagos at the mission had outposts up and down the stream. Runners had brought word of their coming to the mission. As a result, all the Indians from the village were crowded upon the river's edge to welcome them. They were not alone. The Jesuits' helpers, some traders, even Fr. André—all had come to greet them.

Their canoes touched the shore. Fr. André came forward and embraced Fr. Marquette. Tears of joy shone in the older priest's eyes.

"We had given you up for lost, Father," he cried. "And now you are here—thin, and with a fever, if I mistake not, but here."

"It was not God's will that we should fail," said Fr. Marquette. "But first"—he turned to the travelers and Joliet—"follow me."

Fr. Marquette led them to the chapel. There they knelt while he led them in a prayer of thanksgiving. Then Fr. André too led prayers of thanksgiving for their safe return. The Indians, meanwhile, crowding the chapel and milling around outside it, spoke freely of their amazement that the travelers had escaped the monsters of the great river. They believed that this was due solely to the help of the Great Spirit of the white men, and they immediately laid more offerings before the altar of the chapel.

That night, before the council fires in the lodge of the Winnebago chief, the Indians made many long speeches of welcome. They listened to Fr. Marquette's stories of the dangers they had met and passed safely. They urged Joliet to retell each adventure in his own words. After each account from Fr. Marquette and Joliet, the Winnebagos grunted in approval.

It was very late before they were allowed to go

to bed. Only then did Fr. André come to Fr. Marquette with a sealed paper in his hand. "I have something for you, Father," he said. "It came from Father Dablon some time ago. I did not want to give it to you until now, in case the news in it might dim your pleasure at coming back to us."

Fr. Marquette broke the seal and read Fr. Dablon's letter.

Then he learned that he had come home. He had been moved from St. Ignatius to St. Francis Xavier. He would not again have to go into the North.

It was now too well along in autumn for Joliet to think of going to Quebec. He would be caught by snow and ice on the way. He might perish. So he too remained at the mission. Little Fox stayed with him.

All that winter, while Fr. Marquette made a slow recovery from the ill health which had stayed with him ever since the party had turned back from the Arkansas village, the two men worked at their reports.

Fr. Marquette wrote his in the form of a letter to

Fr. Dablon. As he worked, he thought with humble pleasure that his report too might be published, as so many others had been, in the Jesuit *Relations*. It was his reading of these tales of courage that had made him wish to come to these shores.

Joliet's report was longer. It was for Governor Frontenac.

They checked each other's notes and conclusions. And each of them drew a map of their route. When Fr. Marquette put down the name of the great river, he remembered his promise to the Blessed Virgin and named it River of the Conception in her honor.

Little by little during that winter, Fr. Marquette's strength returned. Yet he tired easily, perhaps because he helped with the work of the mission. He baptized the sick and the children. He went out to preach among outlying tribes. But he could not do nearly as much of the mission work as he wanted to do. He had long ago resigned himself to God's will, but he prayed daily for his recovery. And he prayed, too, that he might return to the Illinois Indians, as he had promised.

[167]

By the time winter ended and the birds came back from the South for that spring of 1674, Fr. Marquette had regained much of his strength. He had never been a powerful man. He had never had a fraction of the strength that was Fr. Dablon's, or that which many of the missionaries had. He believed in his heart that his safe return from the journey down the great river was due solely to the protection of the Blessed Virgin.

Late that spring, Fr. Marquette said farewell to Joliet. The ice in the Straits of Michilimackinac had gone out. The passage to the North was clear. He was sad when Joliet left. They had been together for almost a year, and each had come to respect and admire the other.

With Joliet's going, Fr. Marquette's thoughts turned more and more often to the Illinois at Kaskaskia. He knew he was not yet strong enough to travel and to bear again the hardships of a journey into rough country. He was much troubled. He feared that he would not be able to keep his promise to the Illinois Indians—both the settlement at Kaskaskia and the village across the great river.

There were many days when he fell back into his former state of weakness. On such days he had to lie still and refrain from his duties. Though he had the best of care, he improved so slowly that often he was tempted to impatience.

The warm days of summer brought Fr. Marquette new strength, and he began to hope again that time would cure him completely. He began to dream of going into the South to stay with the Illinois. His bad days came less often, and finally not at all. He felt his energy returning as his illness went away.

Finally, early that autumn, he was encouraged by his good health to write to Fr. Dablon and ask his permission to spend the coming winter among the Illinois.

At first, Fr. Dablon did not reply to his request. He wrote instead that he had spoken to Joliet. He told Fr. Marquette that Joliet had been upset in his canoe in the La Chine Rapids of the Ottawa River. Some of his men had died, and Joliet had lost all his precious reports. Fr. Marquette should therefore send up his record of the voyage, but before doing so, should prepare a second copy, so that all would not be lost in case of accident.

Fr. Marquette obediently made a second copy of his account and sent the first copy, together with his maps, with some Indians going to Quebec. Perhaps Joliet might see his account once more and re-write his own. Together with his report, Fr. Marquette sent another letter about his deep desire to bring Christianity to the Illinois.

This time Fr. Dablon gave his consent.

Fr. Marquette's orders came in mid-autumn. At once he began to make ready with the help of Pierre Porteret, who was free to go with him, and another traveler, Jacques Vaquier, whom Porteret had found to make the journey.

10

The Last Months

THEY SET OUT on the twenty-fifth of October. It was just thirteen months since Fr. Marquette had returned from his travels on the great river. The morning was fine and sunny, though clouds lay along the horizon.

They were not long alone. At the Sturgeon Bay portage they met nine canoe-loads of Indians. Four of them were filled with Illinois and five with Pottawattomies. They too were going to Kaskaskia. They invited Fr. Marquette and his paddlers to join them, and they were happy when Fr. Marquette accepted.

The sunny weather of the first few days did not last. Suddenly, without warning, came the cold. And with the cold came icy rain and snow. Time after time, they were forced to put in to shore. There the hardy Indians went off to hunt so that they would have food against the cold. Those who remained raised shelters for Fr. Marquette and the whole party. Some of the Indians held a feast of worship to a wolf skin. This made Fr. Marquette unhappy because some of these same Indians had said they were converts.

There was no lack of game. Turkeys, geese, deer, buffalos—all these were within reach of the hunting Indians. One day, when a howling blizzard all but shut out the sight of Lake Michigan, an Illinois warrior named Chachagwessiou came out of the woods with a dead deer on his shoulders. This he gladly shared with the travelers on shore.

Strong winds often forced them to land. But one day, they were almost prevented from landing by huge blocks of ice. Their canoes were too frail for the rough waters and the towering waves of Lake Michigan. They were river canoes, not the stronger, larger lake craft. Sometimes they lost a day, sometimes two. Once they lost five days.

November went by, with one delay after another. They were still on Lake Michigan. Yet they should long ago have reached the Chicago River and gone inland. The snow and cold persisted.

And even as November slipped away, so did Fr. Marquette's strength. The recovery he had made at St. Francis Xavier was soon lost. By the time December came, he was so weak that he could hardly paddle. Yet he seated himself as usual each day and would not shirk his share of the hard work.

On the fourth of December, they put into the Chicago River. This too was wind-swept. Snow still fell. By this time Fr. Marquette was so ill that his weakness could not be hidden from his two companions. Yet he insisted on going forward.

In four days they reached the place of the portage. But here the river was covered with ice almost six inches thick. They could not go on. It was the feast of the Immaculate Conception and, much to his grief, Fr. Marquette was too ill to say Mass. He had not served at the paddle for two days.

The travelers at once took out their axes and began to cut down trees.

"We must build a cabin as well as we can," explained Porteret, in reply to Fr. Marquette's anxious question.

"Surely we can go on with these friendly Indians," said Fr. Marquette.

"Father, we must stay here," answered Porteret. "It will mean many hardships, but in the spring we may yet reach the village of the Illinois. To go now would mean certain death."

"I welcome death, Pierre. I do not fear it. If it is on my account that you are staying behind, I beg you and Jacques to go on with the Indians. Do not think of me," entreated Fr. Marquette.

"Father, I think of all of us," replied Porteret. "It is not only because of you. We cannot travel like the Indians. We are men of boats and water, not of woods. So we are better off here under a shelter."

The Indians, who were carrying goods brought from the French in exchange for furs, had no choice but to go on. They were greatly worried by Fr. Marquette's illness, and they listened closely when he told them to wait and hold their great council in the spring. He would be with them at that time. They felt bad because they had nothing but food to leave with Fr. Marquette who needed warmth. But soon after they were gone, the white men were able to barter some tobacco with some passing Indians for three large ox skins.

The log cabin grew as rapidly as they could cut and shape the logs. Each of them seemed to know that unless Fr. Marquette were soon under shelter, his frail body would succumb to the bitter weather. They worked tirelessly, and soon they had a shelter against the weather. Though they had no mud with which to block up the cracks between the logs, they used sticks and leaves to good effect. While they did not have a cold-proof shelter, a roaring fire kept them warm.

In this cabin they settled down for the winter.

Many times during that winter, memories of Fr. Marquette's boyhood returned to him. In those early years he had been fired with a zeal for missionary work. He had prayed often that he might reach New France and become a missionary among the Indians. This prayer had been granted. He had prayed too that he might give his life in this work. Often during those cold months, Fr. Marquette was sure that God was preparing to grant this wish too.

It was a hard winter.

Yet they were not often alone for long stretches of time. Parties of hunting Indians stopped now and then and left part of their kill for them. The news that they were there had spread among the Indians. A band of Illinois braves came from Kaskaskia to beg Fr. Marquette to stay in their land for the rest of his life. They brought corn meal, pumpkins, and dried meat. They also carried a dozen beaver skins and a rush mat. In return, Fr. Marquette gave them two double mirrors, some glass beads, some knives, and a hatchet.

These gifts from friendly Indians helped them through the winter.

Early in the following year, when they had been there a month and a half, a white man reached the cabin. He came with an Indian guide from his own cabin almost twenty miles away. He was a French doctor named Antoine Defage.

"The Indians have told me you are sick, Father," he explained. "I have come to do what I can for you. We've brought you some blueberries and corn, and the good wishes of the Illinois who are anxious to see you."

Fr. Marquette thanked him. "I am not yet strong enough to travel. But I am not growing weaker," he said.

Dr. Defage did what he could for Fr. Marquette. When he was ready to go, Fr. Marquette decided to send Jacques Vaquier along with Dr. Defage and his guide to tell the Illinois he would be with them at the spring council, God willing.

When Jacques returned, he brought with him a sack of corn and some buffalo meat. The grateful

Illinois had sent these to the Black Robe and his companions to show how much they looked forward to his coming to live with them. Later that same month, Fr. Marquette was able to send letters to the St. Francis Xavier mission with a party of Illinois moving north. These Indians had camped not far from the cabin and had remained there, hunting, for almost a month.

March came, and with it came the hope of departure.

But the north wind blew without pause. Fr. Marquette and the other men began a novena to the Blessed Virgin, asking that he be permitted to keep his promise and return to start the mission at Kaskaskia before he died.

Not until the last week of March did the wind's direction change. Then one morning late in the month, the wind came out of the South. Almost immediately a different kind of game appeared. With the warmer weather, the first flocks of passenger pigeons flew over. Fr. Marquette joined his companions to shoot thirty of the birds.

The south wind kept blowing steadily. On the

twenty-eighth of March, the ice in the river broke up. Next day the water came so high that it began to enter the cabin. Fr. Marquette and his friends had to pile all their goods in the trees and take refuge on a hill a little distance away.

While they were there, Dr. Defage and his Indian companion came in their canoe and shouted that the waters were rising. They decided at once to start for Kaskaskia. They rescued their goods, put them into the canoe, and set out. Dr. Defage went with them. Fr. Marquette was not yet well, but he was stronger than he had been in December. He knew that though he might begin the mission at Kaskaskia, he would not be able to remain there long.

Once they had passed the portage, where they waded through knee-deep water, and had reached the Des Plaines River, the high waters carried the two canoes rapidly toward their goal.

Eleven days beyond the portage, on a day in early April, Fr. Marquette reached Kaskaskia. Indians that he knew were at the shore to greet him.

He saw Red Feather, who had guided them out to the lake a year and a half ago. He saw once more the old chief, Blue Goose, who was the head of the village. All hailed Fr. Marquette with great pleasure.

They were tender with him. They saw how ill he was. They admired the courage he showed by coming to them when he was so sick.

The village lay well back from the river, among the trees. There were six hundred Illinois families in it. Blue Goose could command fifteen hundred braves and many more hunters who sold guns to the Illinois.

Once again Fr. Marquette allowed himself to be fed. Once more he smoked the peace pipe. Then, after but a single night of rest in the lodge the Illinois had set aside for him, he began his duties.

He went to talk with the elders of Kaskaskia, and he sat in little circles to smoke with them. He spoke with the squaws, who were hard at work weaving rush mats. He talked with the young braves. He was constantly on his feet, walking from lodge to lodge from dawn to dusk. Each day he read Mass and the prayers of his order.

But when Pierre Porteret and Jacques Vaquier came to him one day and told him they must return to Michilimackinac, he said only, "Wait for me."

"You are going back then, Father?" asked Porteret in amazement. "But you are hardly well!"

"I will not be well again, Pierre," said Fr. Marquette calmly. "I want to confess and receive the last sacrament. We will go as soon as I have spoken at the council."

All was not yet ready for the great council. Fr. Marquette began now to give instructions. He chose the older braves for the group meetings. It was necessary first that he find out how they looked upon his teaching. Much to his joy, Fr. Marquette found out that they were ready to believe what he had to say to them. And when he proposed having the great council soon, they were eager to do so. Fr. Marquette knew that this was in part because the Indians liked ceremonies.

To the west of Kaskaskia lay a wide, treeless prairie. This was chosen as the meeting place for

the council. And Easter week was chosen as the
time. Rush mats and deer skins were spread on the
ground there. Fr. Marquette prepared four large
pictures of the Blessed Virgin and pinned them on
pieces of cloth. Then he raised them up on poles,
where all the Illinois could see the smiling face of
Our Lady looking down upon them.

Five hundred chiefs, led by Blue Goose, sat in a
great circle around the priest. They were pressed
by a thousand of the younger braves. Beyond them
sat the squaws and children. Even the dogs gathered
beyond the circle.

There in the sunlight of that day, Fr. Marquette
spoke for the last time to the Illinois. He talked of
the beauty and holiness of the Catholic Faith. He
spoke of his love for the Illinois, saying that he had
come far, though ill, to serve them and bring them
to the Great Spirit who was God. He told of the
glory of France, Defender of the Faith. He gave
to the chiefs the last of the gifts he had with him.

The Indians listened with attention and with
awe.

When Fr. Marquette had finished, old Blue

Goose rose and spoke. "We have heard you, Black Robe. We welcome you among us. We look upon you with the same love that you show us. We are ready to share in the protection of France. We want to hear more of your Great Manitou. We are ready to listen to more of your words. We hope you will stay with us. We hope you will always befriend us."

Fr. Marquette rose weakly to his feet again. "I wish I could stay among you," he said. "But my Father calls to me. I must go. Before the sun has come seven more days, I will be gone. I will return to live among you if I can. I will come back to this misssion of the Immaculate Conception, if it is my Father's will. But if I do not return, another Black Robe will come in my place. He too will be your friend."

On Easter Sunday, Fr. Marquette said Mass under the sunny heavens. The Illinois were gathered about him in such numbers that they crowded the prairie. After the Mass had been said, Fr. Marquette completed his preparations to leave. He sent word to Porteret and Vaquier to be ready.

They set out in the morning. The Illinois did not want him to go. He had to speak to them in the streets of Kaskaskia. He had to promise them that France would not forget them. He had to promise them again on the river bank that the Black Robe would send someone who would tell them more about God. They must treat him with the same kindness they had shown to him. The Illinois brought Fr. Marquette as much food as they could carry in the canoe. Finally, old Blue Goose appointed a group of the Illinois, led by his son, Painted Turtle, to go with the three white men as far as Lake Michigan.

So they started on Fr. Marquette's last journey.

At first Fr. Marquette himself paddled now and then. But the struggle against the current of the Illinois River was too taxing. It only made him weaker to try to paddle. By the time they reached the Des Plaines River, Fr. Marquette lay on his back in the canoe. He murmured his prayers and each day said a rosary. Every night when they made camp, the paddlers carried Fr. Marquette from the canoe and put him down beside the campfire. Then Pierre Porteret read the prayers of Fr. Marquette's order to him. At the portage, Painted Turtle ordered the Indians to carry the canoe with Fr. Marquette in it, so that he need not walk.

At last they reached the lake. There Painted Turtle bade him a sad farewell.

It was May, 1675, and the way before them was long. The men decided to go up toward Michilimackinac by the east coast of Lake Michigan. They were less familiar with this route, but it promised to be shorter. Besides, it was said that the currents along that coast set to the north.

They went around the foot of Lake Michigan and started up the coast. They pushed themselves as hard as they could. Yet, day by day, Fr. Marquette grew weaker. Despite all their attempts, they could not go rapidly. The wind was harsh, and often the waves ran high.

On the eighteenth of May, when they guessed that they were half way up the coast toward Michilimackinac, they passed a small river which emptied into the lake. Beyond it rose a little hill, crowded with oak trees.

"Pierre," said Fr. Marquette in a voice that was hardly more than a whisper, "land here."

Without question, Porteret drove toward the shore.

"I cannot go any farther," explained Fr. Marquette. "Carry me up that little hill. It will make a good place for my grave."

The two men went ahead to build a small shelter, covering it over with bark and branches. It was now evening. They knew that Fr. Marquette had waited until evening before asking them to land, since they would have to camp for the night in any case. By the time they finished the shelter, the dusk was deep, and only a thin line of the sunset shone across the lake in the West.

They came back to the canoe where Fr. Marquette lay patiently. They took him up tenderly and carried him toward the hill. They laid him on a rush mat beside a little fire they had built.

Fr. Marquette gathered his failing strength. He heard the confessions of Porteret and Vaquier. Then he told them how to bury him.

"Do not trouble yourselves too much. Let the

grave be only deep enough to be out of reach of animals. Now go and wait for me to ring this little Mass bell," he said. "I thank you for your gentleness, your kindness, and your patience. Try to sleep a little. If I grow worse, I will ring the bell. I am sorry if I delay you."

The two men walked sorrowfully away.

It was three hours before the bell rang. Close to midnight, the men heard its faint, musical notes, and came running to Fr. Marquette's side. They fell to their knees beside him, crossing themselves.

Fr. Marquette spoke in whispers. "Please, Pierre. Take the crucifix from my neck. Hold it before my eyes."

Porteret did as he had been asked to do.

Fr. Marquette whispered his last prayers. "Mother of God, remember me," he finished.

When his voice could be heard no more, the men thought he had died. Vaquier cried out, "Jesus —Mary!"

Fr. Marquette's eyes flickered open once more. He smiled faintly. "Jesus—Mary," he said clearly.

[187]

Then he closed his eyes for the last time.

He had prayed to be allowed to die in the wilderness. This prayer, like his wish to come to New France and serve God among the Indians, had been answered.

VISION BOOKS

Stories of Great Catholics to Inspire Young Hearts

VISION BOOKS are an exciting new series especially designed to acquaint boys and girls from eight to sixteen with the lives of great Catholic lay figures, martyrs, and saints.

VISION BOOKS will inspire and instruct. Their lively telling, their readability, and their historical accuracy make them unique. These colorful action-filled life stories combine scrupulous fidelity to facts with high entertainment value. Besides giving youngsters a broader understanding of their Faith, this series also brings them a world of information about history and geography, at home and in foreign lands. Through VISION BOOKS young people will better comprehend and visualize the courage and piety that inspired these famous followers of Christ.

VISION BOOKS are written by outstanding authors, each of whom tells the story of the saint or hero closest to his heart.

VISION BOOKS will captivate young readers. These rewarding and inspiring life stories of great Catholics unlock a lavish treasure house of thrilling reading and spiritual adventure.

1. ST. JOHN BOSCO AND THE CHILDREN'S SAINT, DOMINIC SAVIO, by Catherine Beebe. Illustrated by Robb Beebe. *Imprimatur*

Juggler, acrobat, magician, tailor, writer, and teacher— John Bosco became all these in his efforts to lead boys and girls to God. The boyish pranks of Dominic Savio and John Bosco's other pupils keep his school full of noise, laughter, and appeal for young readers.

2. ST. THÉRÈSE AND THE ROSES, by Helen Walker Homan. Illustrated by Harry Schaare and George Thompson. *Imprimatur*

The Little Flower, St. Thérèse of Lisieux, wanted to become the plaything of the Child Jesus. Her home life with her four sisters, her adventures at school, and her efforts to enter the convent produce a story which combines inspirational value with the type of charm found in Alcott's *Little Women*.

3. FATHER MARQUETTE AND THE GREAT RIVERS, by August Derleth. Illustrated by H. Lawrence Hoffman. *Imprimatur*

The thrilling story of Father Marquette who came down from Canada with Louis Joliet, explored the mighty Mississippi River, and braved the dangers of tomahawks and tortures to bring the word of God to the savage Indians in this unknown land.

4. ST. FRANCIS OF THE SEVEN SEAS, by Albert J. Nevins, M.M. Illustrated by Leo Manso. *Imprimatur*

Against the exotic background of the East is told the story of St. Francis Xavier's voyage to India in the sixteenth century, his strange adventures as a missionary, his turbulent conflicts with evil rulers, and his struggles to win the Orient for Jesus Christ.